JAMES C. HANKS

SCHOOL BULLYING
HOW LONG IS THE ARM OF THE LAW?

D1522720

Section of State and
Local Government Law

Cover design by Elmarie Jara/ABA Publishing.

Printed in the United States of America

16 15 14 13   5 4 3 2

Library of Congress Cataloging-in-Publication Data

Hanks, James C., 1950–
    School bullying : how long is the arm of the law? / James C. Hanks.
        p. cm.
    Includes bibliographical references and index.
    ISBN 978-1-61438-627-8 (alk. paper)
  1. Bullying in schools—United States. 2. School discipline—Law and legislation—United States. 3. Harassment in schools—Law and legislation—United States. 4. Bullying—United States—Prevention.
I. Title.
    KF4159.H36   2012
    344.73'0793—dc23

                                                    2012028485

Discounts are available for books ordered in bulk. Special consideration is given to state bars, CLE programs, and other bar-related organizations. Inquire at Book Publishing, ABA Publishing, American Bar Association, 321 North Clark Street, Chicago, Illinois 60654-7598.

www.ShopABA.org

Contents

Acknowledgments

When you write a book and you think about whom you should thank or acknowledge, it is wise to remember your spouse and it is wiser still to remember where she fits in the constellation of stars that have guided your way. So it is appropriate that I begin with my wife, Janet, who has supported and encouraged me in all of my work, including this book. Depending on your point of view, Janet has either endured or reveled in my many absences from the home over the years. I like to think that I am wise enough not to ask which sentiment better captures her feelings. I know that I am wise enough to thank her either way.

Some things that we do are the product of the inspiration of another. This book is one of those things. The inspiration for it came from Tamara Edmonds Askew, the very able and creative director of the American Bar Association's Section of State and Local Government Law. My thanks go to Tamara and to Marti Chumbler, the section's publications director, for their encouragement and support of my efforts.

I was privileged to be able to make a presentation at the 2011 Annual Meeting of the American Bar Association on the subject of cyberbullying. That privilege was greatly enhanced by the quality of the speakers who joined me in that presentation. I learned from them and about them, and that learning was valuable to me in the work that I did on this book. I wish to thank Grant Bowers (counsel to the Toronto District School Board in Toronto, Ontario), Dr. Jeff Gardere (adjunct clinical professor at Touro College of Osteopathic Medicine in New York City), and Kathy Macdonald (constable with the Calgary Police Service in Calgary, Alberta). Each of them in their own way made our presentation a very special memory for me.

The leadership of the Section of State and Local Government Law has devoted countless hours to an expansion of the work that we do in the section, striving to create and provide more material to better serve a wider audience. That wider audience includes lawyers with either a professional or a personal interest in education law. I appreciate the opportunity to help fill some of the need in this area. I wish to acknowledge the support of section leaders past and present who have supported the work of the Public Education Committee.

One of the advantages of being older is that sometimes younger people will help you do things that you cannot do or that you choose not to do because it would force you to admit that you can no longer run fast enough to keep up with the pace of change. I owe great thanks for their research, review, and commentary to two such younger people, Kristy Latta and Miriam Van Heukelem, associates in my law firm.

The members of my law firm have been unfailing in their support of my work in the Section of State and Local Government Law. All bar association work is a commitment of time and resources that is difficult to make without the backing of those with whom you practice law. I thank my firm for having my back. Although I have said before that I am blessed to work for Ahlers & Cooney, I need to say it again.

Finally, I wish to thank Leslie Keros, associate editor, and the staff of the ABA for their help in making this book a reality. I once thought that I knew a little bit about writing a book. Now I know how little I know.

About the Author

James C. Hanks is a member of the Local Government Law and Employment Law departments of Ahlers & Cooney, P.C., in Des Moines, Iowa. He is the Vice-Chair of the American Bar Association Section of State and Local Government Law and is a member of the ABA Section of Labor and Employment Law. He is also a member of the Iowa State Bar Association and the Nebraska State Bar Association. He formerly chaired the National School Boards Association Council of School Attorneys, the Iowa Council of School Board Attorneys, and the Iowa State Bar Association Labor Law Committee. He has served as lecturer on education or employment law issues for the University of Iowa College of Law, the National School Boards Association, the National Organization for Legal Problems in Education, the American Bar Association, the National Association of State Boards of Education, the National Public Employers Labor Relations Association, and the Iowa, Nebraska, Kansas, and Michigan Councils of School Attorneys. He is the editor and contributing author of *School Violence* (ABA 2004) and the author of *Recent Developments in Education Law: Regulating Student Speech in Cyberspace*, published in *The Urban Lawyer* (Summer 2011); *The Bully at School Goes High Tech: The Legal Issues*, 2011 ABA Section of State and Local Government Law; *Employment at Will*, NSBA Council of School Attorneys Annual Proceedings, 1984; *Fair Labor Standards Act Amendments of 1985, Inquiry and Analysis*, NSBA Council of School Attorneys, May 1987; and *Ethics and the School Board Lawyer*, NSBA Council of School Attorneys Annual Proceedings, 1995. He attended the University of Iowa and received his B.A. in 1972 and his J.D., with high distinction, in 1975. He is a member of Phi Beta Kappa and in 1972 was nominated by the University of Iowa for a Rhodes Scholarship.

Introduction

One measure of the scope of a problem is the attention that it attracts from society in general and from the government in particular. Based on that measure, bullying is a problem of monumental proportions.

All facets of society have embraced antibullying as a cause. A documentary film called *Bully*, released in 2012, follows the lives of five students who were bullied; two of the students killed themselves. The content of *Bully* is provocative, but the Motion Picture Association of America changed its rating from R to PG-13 due to the protests of people who wanted a wider audience to see—and benefit from—the movie.[1] Beyond the movie, there are support groups, programs, websites, and campaigns on Facebook all focused on the problem of bullying.[2] The news media regularly reports on incidents of bullying, such as the Tyler Clementi suicide and the recent conviction of his room-

---

1. Bully, Now Playing, Official Site, http://thebullyproject.com/indexflash.html (last visited June 14, 2012).

2. *See, e.g.*, Bullying Support Groups, http://www.overcomebullying.org/bullying-support-groups.html#LocalYouthSchoolBullying (last visited June 14, 2012); Dakarai I. Aarons, *Efforts to End Bullying, a Challenge to Leaders, Gain New Momentum*, EDUC. WK.: SPOTLIGHT ON BULLYING, May 12, 2010; U.S. Dep't of Health and Human Services, stopbullying.gov, http://www.stopbullying.gov/ (last visited June 14, 2012); Facebook, Stop Bullying: Speak Up, http://www.facebook.com/stopbullyingspeakup (last visited June 14, 2012).

mate, and celebrities have been prominent in campaigning against it.[3]

The government, too, has become involved in the problem of bullying. In August of 2010, the U.S. Department of Education, the U.S. Department of Health and Human Services, and four other federal departments held the first-ever

---

3. Reports concerning incidents of bullying at school are widespread. *See, e.g.*, Michelle Nicks, WFMJ, Wellsville Mother Speaks Out Against Bullying, After Son Tries to Take His Own Life (Mar. 22, 2012), http://www.wfmj.com/story/17234194/wellsville-mother-speak-out-against-bullying-after-son-tried-to-take-his-own-life; Carrie Wood, *Bullying Incidents on the Rise in Lake Washington School District*, KIRKLAND REP., Feb. 24, 2010, *available at* http://www.kirklandreporter.com/news/85094287.html; Peter Schworm & Milton J. Valencia, *Anger Turns Toward Staff in Bullying Case*, BOSTON GLOBE, Mar. 31, 2010, *available at* http://www.boston.com/news/local/massachusetts/articles/2010/03/31/anger_turns_toward_school_staff_in_bullying_case/; Jason Schultz, *Palm Beach County Reports Most School Bullying Incidents, Though Numbers Might be Skewed*, PALM BEACH POST, July 20, 2011, *available at* http://www.palmbeachpost.com/news/schools/palm-beach-county-reports-most-school-bullying-incidents-1624781.html?sort=desc. Such reports often involve lawsuits filed against school districts. *See, e.g.*, Steve McConnell, *Bullying Federal Lawsuit Lodged Against Scranton School District Headed to Settlement Talks*, SCRANTON TIMES-TRIB., Mar. 23, 2012, *available at* http://thetimes-tribune.com/news/bullying-federal-lawsuit-suit-lodged-against-scranton-school-district-headed-to-settlement-talks-1.1289388#axzz1r0uyO78t; Steve Williams, Care2, Sixth Bullied Student Sues Minnesota School District (Aug. 13, 2011), http://www.care2.com/causes/sixth-bullied-student-sues-minnesota-school-district.html. The Tyler Clementi case received considerable media attention. *See, e.g.*, Joseph Ax & Jessica Dye, Reuters, Rutgers Hate Crime Verdict Sends Anti-Bullying Message (Mar. 17, 2012), http://www.reuters.com/article/2012/03/17/us-crime-rutgers-analysis-idUSBRE82G04B20120317. On celebrity campaigns, see John Mitchell, PopEater, Celebrities Team Up for Anti-Bullying Campaigns (Oct. 6, 2010), http://www.popeater.com/2010/10/06/tim-gunn-ellen-degeneres-bullying-psa/.

National Bullying Summit to bring together state, local, civic, and corporate leaders to plan a strategy to end bullying.[4] Then, on March 10, 2011, President Barack Obama and First Lady Michelle Obama convened the White House Conference on Bullying Prevention.[5] As part of a follow-up to the conference, the White House launched a website to collect resources to combat bullying: www.stopbullying.gov.[6]

Despite the societal and governmental attention being paid to the problem, bullying persists. Survey results released in October 2010 by the Josephson Institute Center for Youth Ethics revealed that in the year preceding the survey, 47 percent of the 43,321 high school students surveyed reported being bullied (physically abused, teased, or taunted in a way that upset them), and 50 percent admitted to bullying someone else.[7] The Sioux City Community

---

4. *See* Press Release, U.S. Dep't of Educ., U.S. Education Secretary to Keynote Department's First-Ever Bullying Summit: Partners Will Come Together to Develop a National Strategy for Reducing and Ending Bullying (Aug. 2010), *available at* http://www.ed.gov/news/media-advisories/us-education-secretary-keynote-departments-first-ever-bullying-summit.

5. President Obama and the First Lady at the White House Conference on Bullying Prevention, WHITEHOUSE.GOV, Mar. 10, 2011 [hereinafter White House Conference], *available at* http://www.whitehouse.gov/photos-and-video/video/2011/03/10/president-obama-first-lady-conference-bullying-prevention#transcript.

6. U.S. Dep't of Health and Human Services, stopbullying.gov, http://www.stopbullying.gov/.

7. Press Release, Josephson Inst., Ctr. for Youth Ethics, The Ethics of American Youth: 2010; Largest Study Ever Shows Half of All High School Students Were Bullies and Nearly Half Were the Victims of Bullying During Past Year (Oct. 26, 2010), *available at* http://charactercounts.org/programs/reportcard/2010/installment01_report-card_bullying-youth-violence.html.

School District—former home to Alex Libby, one of the five students in *Bully*—partnered with the Waitt Institute for Violence Prevention more than twelve years ago to create an antibullying program; even with this program in place and training for staff, Libby was bullied to the point where his family decided to move.[8]

The consequences of this persistent problem are always painful. As he said in his remarks at the White House conference, President Obama himself felt the effects of bullying: "[W]ith big ears and the name that I have, I wasn't immune. I didn't emerge unscathed."[9] Similarly, millions of students feel the pain and remember it for years. A long and persistent memory apparently led Eric Giray to sue his former classmate Daniel Dworakowski and former school (Calhoun School) for an act of what he alleges was bullying. The lawsuit was filed in the Manhattan Supreme Court in March 2012. The alleged incident took place on October 15, 2004.[10]

Sometimes the consequences are tragic. Tragedy can sometimes mean the need to relocate to another school or another town, as in the case of Libby. But tragedy can take its cruelest turn in the form of suicide:

---

8. Perry Beeman, *Victims of Bullying, Including Iowa Boy, Featured in Movie*, DES MOINES REG. 1A, 6A (Mar. 31, 2012), *available at* http://www.desmoinesregister.com/article/20120331/NEWS/303310024/ Victims-bullying-including-Iowa-boy-featured-documentary.

9. White House Conference, *supra* note 5.

10. Barbara Ross, *He Sues School and Student Bully—8 Yrs. Later!* N.Y. DAILY NEWS (Mar. 22, 2012), *available at* http://articles.nydaily news.com/2012-03-22/news/31227186_1_anti-bullying-policy-elephant-ears-administrators.

Megan Meier was 13 years old when she committed suicide due to bullying from a fellow classmate and her mother through a fake MySpace account. 18 year old Rutgers University student Tyler Clementi jumped from the George Washington Bridge after footage of him engaged in sexual activity was secretly recorded and released online by his roommates. Hope Witsell committed suicide in 2009 after being taunted by classmates for a nude photo she sent to a crush that others found.[11]

Beyond its effect on individual students, bullying has a decided effect on the entire educational community. Recognizing the wide and profound impact of bullying on the school environment, the U.S. Court of Appeals for the Fourth Circuit observed that schools have an obligation to protect their students, an obligation that outweighs free speech concerns:

According to a federal government initiative, student-on-student bullying is a "major concern" in schools across the country and can cause victims to become depressed and anxious, to be afraid to go to school, and to have thoughts of suicide. Just as schools have a responsibility to provide a safe environment for students free from messages advocating illegal drug use, schools have a duty to

---

11. Jessica Kolifrath, All News Wire, Cyberbullying: The Hate, Torment and Death Virus (Oct. 28, 2010), www.allnewswire.com/cyber bullying.

protect their students from harassment and bullying in the school environment. Far from being a situation where school authorities "suppress speech on political and social issues based on disagreement with the viewpoint expressed," school administrators must be able to prevent and punish harassment and bullying in order to provide a safe school environment conducive to learning.[12]

Since public education remains a responsibility of the states and their units of local government—the school administrators who have the obligation to prevent and punish bullying work for local school districts—the primary response of the law thus far has been at the state and local level: the adoption of statutes and state or local policies. This monograph will review state statutes concerning bullying, discuss the constitutional issues that have arisen or that may arise from the application of antibullying regulations, examine the cases in which school district regulation of bullying has been addressed, review the existing federal guidance that is relevant to bullying, and offer some suggestions for a systemic approach to bullying.

---

12. Kowalski v. Berkeley County Schools, 652 F.3d 565, 572 (4th Cir. 2011) (citations omitted).

State Statutes

An examination of how state statutes have handled the issue of bullying highlights a diverse range of treatment of not only the definitions and scope of the statutes but also the procedures employed by the states in crafting their antibullying legislation.

A. Definitions and Scope

On March 19, 2012, South Dakota became the forty-ninth state to enact legislation prohibiting bullying in schools.[1] Now, only the state of Montana has no law on the subject.[2] A key to understanding all of the state statutes is their definition of *bullying* and the scope of the application of those definitions.[3]

---

1. S. 130, 87th Leg. (S.D. 2012).

2. *See* SAMEER HINDUJA & JUSTIN W. PATCHIN, CYBERBULLYING RESEARCH CTR., STATE CYBERBULLYING LAWS, A BRIEF REVIEW OF STATE CYBERBULLYING LAWS AND POLICIES (Feb. 2012) (collecting state statutes on the topic of cyberbullying).

3. *See generally* Natasha Rose Manuel, *Cyber-Bullying: Its Recent Emergence and Needed Legislation to Protect Adolescent Victims*, LOY. J. PUB. INT. L., Fall 2011, at 219; Philip T.K. Daniel, *Bullying and Cyberbullying in Schools: An Analysis of Student Free Expression, Zero Tolerance Policies, and State Anti-Harassment Legislation*, 268 EDUC. L. REP. 619 (2011); Susan Hanley Kosse &

For definitional purposes, the critical elements to assess in any law are (1) the specific conduct that is prohibited; (2) whether the prohibited conduct is a single act or a repeated series of acts; (3) the groups or classes of students that are protected; (4) the inclusion or omission of cyberbullying, or bullying by electronic communication; and (5) the scope of the application of the definition, i.e., whether the statute regulates conduct that is traditionally referred to as "off-campus."

1. Specific Conduct Prohibited

Although it is easy to agree that bullying should be prohibited, it is very challenging to create a definition of *bullying* that is sufficiently specific to withstand a void for vagueness claim, narrowly tailored enough to survive a claim that the definition is overly broad, and respectful of the First Amendment freedom of speech and freedom of religion rights that public school students enjoy. In the rush to fill a gap in the law, legislatures do not always pay as much attention to these restrictions as the courts will require. The result is that there are well-intentioned statutes that have been drafted in a way that will expose the laws to constitutional challenges when they are invoked, particularly when the nature of the bullying is a statement or some form of expressive conduct.

Robert H. Wright, *How Best to Confront the Bully: Should Title IX or Anti-Bullying Statutes Be the Answer?*, 12 DUKE J. GENDER L. & POL'Y, Spring 2005, at 53.

A review of state antibullying statutes in Massachusetts, Georgia, South Dakota, Oregon, and Nevada uncovers several different approaches to the definitional issue.

a. Massachusetts

After the suicide in 2010 of Phoebe Prince, a student who was a victim of bullying at her high school in Hadley, the state of Massachusetts adopted a statute that defines *bullying* similar to the way many other states have defined it:

> "Bullying," the repeated use by one or more students of a written, verbal or electronic expression or a physical act or gesture or any combination thereof, directed at a victim that: (i) causes physical or emotional harm to the victim or damage to the victim's property; (ii) places the victim in reasonable fear of harm to himself or of damage to his property; (iii) creates a hostile environment at school for the victim; (iv) infringes on the rights of the victim at school; or (v) materially and substantially disrupts the education process or the orderly operation of a school. For the purposes of this section, bullying shall include cyberbullying.[4]

---

4. MASS. GEN. LAWS ANN. ch. 71, § 37O(a).

Like most definitions of *bullying*, the Massachusetts version first describes the conduct or communication that is the means by which bullying occurs—"written, verbal or electronic expression or a physical act or gesture or any combination thereof"—and then links that conduct or communication to an impact on a victim. The last sentence of the definition expressly declares that cyberbullying is included in the types of conduct and communication that are being regulated.

The statute then specifies five different consequences that will qualify the conduct or communication as bullying. Of these five consequences, the two most likely to be challenged as vague or overbroad are "causes . . . emotional harm to the victim" and "infringes on the rights of the victim at school." Challenges would emanate from constitutional issues arising from the mandates of the due process clause:

> Due process is designed to ensure fundamental fairness in interactions between individuals and the state. Among other things, the Due Process Clause prohibits enforcement of vague statutes under the void-for-vagueness doctrine. There are three generally cited underpinnings of the void-for-vagueness doctrine. First, a statute cannot be so vague that it does not give persons of ordinary understanding fair notice that certain conduct is prohibited. Second, due process requires that statutes provide those clothed with authority suffi-

cient guidance to prevent the exercise of power in an arbitrary or discriminatory fashion. Third, a statute cannot sweep so broadly as to prohibit substantial amounts of constitutionally-protected activities, such as speech protected under the First Amendment.[5]

In the case of each of the five consequences, the legal issue will be whether the accused has been given fair notice of what conduct or communication is impermissible. How does a student know whether a statement will cause emotional harm to another student? How do students know what constitutes the "rights" of another student on which they may not infringe? How much conduct and how many statements that are constitutionally permissible will be swept up in the prohibitions?

If Student A is a devout member of a religion that considers homosexuality to be a sin, is Student A prohibited from making a statement to another student regarding the tenets of Student A's faith? What if Student A goes to school and wears a T-shirt with the slogan "Be Happy, Not Gay" on it? In fact, this happened in a school district within the U.S. Court of Appeals for the Seventh Circuit, and Judge Posner and his colleagues determined that Student A would be engaging in communication protected under the First Amendment.[6]

---

5. State v. Nail, 743 N.W.2d 535, 539 (Iowa 2007).
6. Zamecnik v. Indian Prairie Sch. Dist. No. 204, 636 F.3d 874 (7th Cir. 2011).

If Student B tells Student C that she dislikes him, will Student B violate the law if Student C is emotionally upset? How much must Student C's feelings be hurt in order for Student C to suffer emotional harm? How will Student B know what Student C's level of tolerance is?

b. Georgia

The antibullying law in Georgia has a narrower definition. That law provides the following definition:

> As used in this Code section, the term "bullying" means an act which occurs on school property, on school vehicles, at designated school bus stops, or at school related functions or activities, or by use of data or software that is accessed through a computer, computer system, computer network, or other electronic technology of a local school system, that is: (1) Any willful attempt or threat to inflict injury on another person, when accompanied by an apparent present ability to do so; or (2) Any intentional display of force such as would give the victim reason to fear or expect immediate bodily harm; or (3) Any intentional written, verbal, or physical act, which a reasonable person would perceive as being intended to threaten, harass, or intimidate, that: (A) Causes another person substantial physical harm within the meaning of Code Section 16-5-23.1 or visible bodily harm as such term is defined in Code Section 16-5-23.1; (B) Has

the effect of substantially interfering with a student's education; (C) Is so severe, persistent, or pervasive that it creates an intimidating or threatening educational environment; or (D) Has the effect of substantially disrupting the orderly operation of the school.[7]

As is the case with the law in Massachusetts, the anti-bullying statute first lists the means by which a student may engage in prohibited bullying. Those means are then described using words requiring proof that the student intends to cause harm to another student and either proof that the harm can be effected or proof that the victim had reason to expect to be harmed:

- "Any willful attempt or threat to inflict injury on another person, when accompanied by an apparent present ability to do so"
- "Any intentional display of force such as would give the victim reason to fear or expect immediate bodily harm"
- "Any intentional written, verbal, or physical act, which a reasonable person would perceive as being intended to threaten, harass, or intimidate"

The consequences are also described in terms indicating that the impact on the victim must be something more than minor:

---

7. GA. CODE ANN. § 20-2-751.4(a).

- "Causes another person substantial physical harm within the meaning of Code Section 16-5-23.1 or visible bodily harm as such term is defined in Code Section 16-5-23.1"
- "Has the effect of substantially interfering with a student's education"
- "Is so severe, persistent, or pervasive that it creates an intimidating or threatening educational environment"
- "Has the effect of substantially disrupting the orderly operation of the school"

However, even the narrower standards adopted by the state of Georgia may be challenged for vagueness if the ordinary student is not able to determine what conduct or communication produces an intimidating or threatening educational atmosphere.

c. South Dakota

The newly adopted law in South Dakota contains a similarly narrow definition of bullying:

> Bullying is a pattern of repeated conduct that causes physical hurt or psychological distress on one or more students that may include threats, intimidation, stalking as defined in chapter 22-19A, physical violence, theft, destruction of property, any threatening use of data or computer software, written or verbal communication, or conduct directed against a student that: (1) Places a student

in reasonable fear of harm to his or her person or damage to his or her property; and either (2) Substantially interferes with a student's educational performance; or (3) Substantially disrupts the orderly operation of a school.[8]

The acts and communications prohibited by the South Dakota law are only those that create in the student a reasonable fear of harm or that substantially interfere with the student's educational performance or with the school's operation. The challenge in this statute is in determining what conduct or communication "interferes with a student's educational performance."

d. Oregon

In the Oregon anti-bullying statute, the definition of *bullying* has four basic components: (1) the act must substantially interfere with a student's educational benefits, opportunities or performance; (2) the act must take place on or immediately adjacent to school grounds, at any school-sponsored activity, on school-provided transportation or at any official school bus stop; (3) the act must physically harm a student or damage a student's property, knowingly place a student in reasonable fear of physical harm to the student or damage to the student's property, or create a hostile educational environment or interfere with the psychological well-being of a student; and (4) the act may be based

---

8. S. Bill No. 130, § 2 (S.D. 87th Sess. Legis. Assemb. 2012).

on, but not be limited to, the protected class status of a person.[9] As is the case with other state statutes, the issue that may arise in Oregon is whether ordinary students will be able to determine the impact of their conduct or communication on the psychological well-being of another student.

e. Nevada

The most restrictive definition of *bullying* appears to be the one in the Nevada statute. In Nevada, a student is guilty of bullying only if the student knowingly threatens "to cause bodily harm or death to a pupil" with the intent to "[i]ntimidate, harass, frighten, alarm, or distress" the pupil; "[c]ause panic or civil unrest"; or "[i]nterfere with the operation of a public school."[10]

Although the terms *frighten*, *alarm*, and *distress* may be vague and subject to attack, the statute's requirement that the bully threaten to cause bodily harm or death to a student will likely be sufficient to permit a prosecution for bullying to survive.

2. Single Act or Series of Acts

There is no universal agreement among the states with regard to whether the definition of *bullying* can be met with a single act or whether repeated acts or a pattern of conduct is necessary.

---

9. OR. REV. STAT. § 339.351(2).

10. NEV. REV. STAT. § 392.915(1).

Some state statutes specifically note that a single incident will be considered bullying. The New Jersey Anti-Bullying Bill of Rights Act, for example, contains definitions identifying the specific conduct that is prohibited and states that "'[h]arassment, intimidation or bullying' means any gesture, any written, verbal or physical act, or any electronic communication, *whether it be a single incident or a series of incidents. . . .*"[11] Other states use similar phrases prohibiting even a single act of bullying, including Kansas ("[a]ny intentional gesture or any intentional written, verbal, electronic or physical act");[12] New Hampshire ("a single significant incident or a pattern of incidents");[13] Georgia ("the term 'bullying' means an act");[14] and Iowa ("any electronic, written, verbal, or physical act or conduct").[15]

Other state statutes specify that bullying involves more than one incident. Such statutes likely reflect the legislative concern that antibullying laws should focus on patterns of behavior, not single episodes of misconduct. The Massachusetts statute, for example, defines *bullying* as "the repeated use by one or more students of a written, verbal or electronic expression or a physical act or gesture or any combination thereof."[16] The requirement of something

---

11. N.J. REV. STAT. § 18A:37-14 (emphasis added).
12. KAN. STAT. ANN. § 72-8256(a)(1).
13. N.H. REV. STAT. § 193-F:3(I)(a).
14. GA. CODE ANN. § 20-2-751.4(a).
15. IOWA CODE § 280.28(2)(b).
16. MASS. GEN. LAWS ANN. ch. 71, § 37O(a).

more than a single act is not unique to Massachusetts. States that require something more than a single act include Florida ("systematically and chronically inflicting hurt or psychological distress")[17] and South Dakota ("[b]ullying is a pattern of repeated conduct").[18]

3. Categories or Classes of Students Protected

The categories of students that are protected under the various antibullying statutes vary widely. On the most liberal end of the continuum are states like New Jersey ("any actual or perceived characteristic, such as race, color, religion, ancestry, national origin, gender, sexual orientation, gender identity and expression, or a mental, physical or sensory disability, or by any other distinguishing characteristic");[19] Iowa ("any actual or perceived trait or characteristic of the student," which include, but are not limited to "age, color, creed, national origin, race, religion, marital status, sex, sexual orientation, gender identity, physical attributes, physical or mental ability or disability, ancestry, political party preference, political belief, socioeconomic status, or familial status");[20] Florida ("[t]he school district bullying and harassment policy shall afford all students the same protection regardless of their status under the

---

17. FLA. STAT. ANN. § 1006.147(3)(a).
18. S. Bill No. 130, § 2 (S.D. 87th Sess. Legis. Assemb. 2012).
19. N.J. REV. STAT. § 18A:37-14.
20. IOWA CODE § 280.28(2)(b)–(c).

law");[21] and New Hampshire ("all students are protected regardless of their status under the law").[22]

Other states have a more limited list of protected categories, such as Oregon ("'[p]rotected class' means a group of persons distinguished, or perceived to be distinguished, by race, color, religion, sex, sexual orientation, national origin, marital status, familial status, source of income or disability").[23] A number of states do not list any categories at all.[24] And South Dakota's law takes a different approach, providing that "no school district policy prohibiting bullying, whether it is existing or adopted pursuant to this Act, may contain any protected classes of students."[25]

4. Inclusion or Omission of Cyberbullying

Cyberbullying is often included in state antibullying statutes. In all, there are fourteen states that specifically include cyberbullying in their statutes (Arkansas, California, Connecticut, Hawaii, Kansas, Louisiana, Massachusetts, Missouri, Nevada, New Hampshire, North Carolina, Oregon, Utah, and Washington); six states in which an amendment or expansion to include cyberbullying has been proposed (Georgia, Illinois, Kentucky, Maine, Nebraska, and

---

21. FLA. STAT. ANN. § 1006.147(4).

22. N.H. REV. STAT. § 193-F:4(II)(c).

23. OR. REV. STAT. § 339.351(3).

24. *See, e.g.*, GA. CODE ANN. § 20-2-751.4; KAN. STAT. ANN. § 72-8256; MASS. GEN. LAWS ANN. ch. 71, § 37O; NEV. REV. STAT. § 392.915.

25. S. Bill No. 130, § 1 (S.D. 87th Sess. Legis. Assemb. 2012).

New York); and thirty-nine states that prohibit electronic harassment.[26]

The Massachusetts statute contains a very comprehensive definition of *cyberbullying*:

"Cyber-bullying," bullying through the use of technology or any electronic communication, which shall include, but shall not be limited to, any transfer of signs, signals, writing, images, sounds, data or intelligence of any nature transmitted in whole or in part by a wire, radio, electromagnetic, photo electronic or photo optical system, including, but not limited to, electronic mail, internet communications, instant messages or facsimile communications. Cyber-bullying shall also include (i) the creation of a web page or blog in which the creator assumes the identity of another person or (ii) the knowing impersonation of another person as the author of posted content or messages, if the creation or impersonation creates any of the conditions enumerated in clauses (i) to (v), inclusive, of the definition of bullying. Cyber-bullying shall also include the distribution by electronic means of a communication to more than one person or the posting of material on an electronic medium that may be accessed by one or more persons, if

---

26. HINDUJA & PATCHIN, *supra* note 2; S. Bill No. 130, § 1 (S.D. 87th Sess. Legis. Assemb. 2012).

the distribution or posting creates any of the conditions enumerated in clauses (i) to (v), inclusive,
of the definition of bullying.[27]

This definition of *cyberbullying* is unique because it includes the use of fake web pages and the impersonation of
the identity of another person. The creation of a fake web
page was the factual foundation for both *Layshock v. Hermitage School District*, in which Layshock, a senior student, used a computer at his grandmother's home during
nonschool hours to create a parody of the high school principal on Myspace.com, and *J.S. v. Blue Mountain School
District*, in which J.S. and a fellow middle school student
created a fake MySpace profile for their principal, identifying him as a bisexual and a pedophile.[28]

The broad definition of the term *electronic communication* appears in many statutes and may render meaning-
less the distinction between cyberbullying and bullying by
electronic communication. For example, New Jersey does
not specifically prohibit cyberbullying, but it does prohibit
any electronic communication that is an act of bullying and
it defines *electronic communication* to mean "a communication transmitted by means of an electronic device, including, but not limited to, a telephone, cellular phone,
computer, or pager."[29] Similarly, the Iowa statute prohibits

---

27. MASS. GEN. LAWS ANN. ch. 71, § 37O(a).
28. Layshock v. Hermitage School District, 650 F.3d 205 (3d Cir.
2011); J.S. v. Blue Mountain School District, 650 F.3d 915 (3d Cir. 2011).
29. N.J. REV. STAT. § 18A:37-14.

electronic bullying, and it defines *electronic* to mean "any communication involving the transmission of information by wire, radio, optical cable, electromagnetic, or other similar means. 'Electronic' includes but is not limited to communication via electronic mail, internet-based communications, pager service, cell phones, and electronic text messaging."[30]

5. Scope of the Application of the Definition

Another feature of antibullying statutes that is likely to invite judicial review is the application of the bullying prohibition to conduct or communication that takes place off campus. Only eight states (Arkansas, Connecticut, Louisiana, Massachusetts, New Hampshire, New Jersey, New York, and South Dakota) include off-campus behavior in their prohibition against bullying.[31]

The right of a school district to regulate student conduct is generally limited to school property and school-related events. In order for the reach of the school district to extend any further, most courts require a showing that the conduct or communication that the district seeks to discipline has an adverse effect on school operations. *Thomas v. Board of Education, Granville Central School District*[32] has been frequently cited for the guidance that the

---

30. Iowa Code § 280.28((2)(a).
31. *Supra* note 26.
32. 607 F.2d 1043 (2d Cir. 1979).

court provided in ruling that the First Amendment rendered a school district powerless to regulate an off-campus newspaper:

> When school officials are authorized only to punish speech on school property, the student is free to speak his mind when the school day ends. In this manner, the community is not deprived of the salutary effects of expression, and educational authorities are free to establish an academic environment in which the teaching and learning process can proceed free of disruption. Indeed, our willingness to grant school officials substantial autonomy within their academic domain rests in part on the confinement of that power within the metes and bounds of the school itself.[33]

However, since the U.S. Supreme Court recently denied certiorari in the *Blue Mountain School District* and *Hermitage School District* cases that were decided by the U.S. Court of Appeals for the Third Circuit, there is no guidance from the highest court with regard to the off-campus application of the First Amendment teachings of *Tinker v. Des Moines Independent Community School District*[34] to bullying. States that choose to expand the reach of their anti-bullying laws will need to justify the intrusion into the homes and private lives of their students and will likely

---

33. *Id.* at 1052.
34. 393 U.S. 503 (1969).

need to focus their attention on the impact that the prohibited conduct or communication has had within the school environment.[35]

a. Massachusetts

In its statement of prohibition against bullying, the Massachusetts statute anticipates the question of nexus between the conduct or communication that it seeks to prohibit and the operation of the school:

> Bullying shall be prohibited: (i) on school grounds, property immediately adjacent to school grounds, at a school-sponsored or school-related activity, function or program whether on or off school grounds, at a school bus stop, on a school bus or other vehicle owned, leased or used by a school district or school, or through the use of technology or an electronic device owned, leased or used by a school district or school and (ii) at a location, activity, function or program that is not school-related, or through the use of technology or an electronic device that is not owned, leased or used by a school district or school, if the bullying creates a hostile environment at school for the victim,

---

35. For further discussion of the need for guidance with respect to the application of the First Amendment to student speech occurring off school premises, see generally Philip T.K. Daniel & Scott Greytak, *A Need to Sharpen the First Amendment Contours of Off-Campus Student Speech*, 273 EDUC. L. REP. 21 (2011).

infringes on the rights of the victim at school or materially and substantially disrupts the education process or the orderly operation of a school. Nothing contained herein shall require schools to staff any non-school related activities, functions, or programs.[36]

The reach of the law to off-campus activities requires a showing of more than just bullying; it requires the additional showing of a connection between the bullying and the school environment: a hostile environment at school, infringement of the rights of the victim at school, or substantial disruption of education or the school. This additional showing may be sufficient to rebut a claim that the school district is without jurisdiction to punish the off-campus behavior.

b. South Dakota

In its newly adopted law, the South Dakota legislature included a provision stating that "[n]either the physical location nor the time of day of any incident involving the use of computers or other electronic devices is a defense to any disciplinary action taken by a school district for conduct determined to meet the definition of bullying in section 2 of this Act."[37] This provision is novel in its wording ("[n]either the physical location nor the time of day of any incident")

---

36. MASS. GEN. LAWS ANN. ch. 71, § 37O(b).
37. S. Bill No. 130, § 5 (S.D. 87th Sess. Legis. Assemb. 2012).

and the fact that those words reach all electronic communication wherever and whenever it occurs. Although this
statement does not require a link to or effect upon the
school, it does refer to the definition of *bullying*, which includes the requirement that the prohibited conduct "(1)
[p]laces a student in reasonable fear of harm to his or her
person or damage to his or her property; and either (2)
[s]ubstantially interferes with a student's educational performance; or (3) [s]ubstantially disrupts the orderly operation of a school."[38] Thus, electronic communications that
take place off school grounds, after school hours, and un-
connected to any school activity may constitute bullying
only if they either substantially interfere with a student's educational performance or substantially disrupt the orderly
operation of a school. By referring to the definition of *bullying*, the statute incorporates a connection to school gov-
ernance that should satisfy a court's search for nexus.

B. Procedures

Following the Tyler Clementi suicide, the New Jersey state
legislature amended its existing antibullying law and made
it what the *New York Times* called "the toughest legislation
against bullying in the nation."[39] The toughness of the Anti-

38. *Id.* § 2.

39. Winnie Hu, *Bullying Law Puts New Jersey Schools on Spot*,
N.Y. TIMES, Aug. 30, 2011, *available at* http://www.nytimes.com/2011/08/
31/nyregion/bullying-law-puts-new-jersey-schools-on-spot.html?_r=1&
pagewanted=all#.

Bullying Bill of Rights Act, as it is known, is derived in large part from its procedures. Many antibullying statutes require local school districts to adopt a policy prohibiting bullying. New Jersey's Anti-Bullying Bill of Rights Act does so as well, but the law does so much more comprehensively than most statutes by identifying twelve separate policy components:

(1) a statement prohibiting harassment, intimidation or bullying of a student;

(2) a definition of harassment, intimidation or bullying no less inclusive than that set forth in [the law];

(3) a description of the type of behavior expected from each student;

(4) consequences and appropriate remedial action for a person who commits an act of harassment, intimidation or bullying;

(5) a procedure for reporting an act of harassment, intimidation or bullying, including a provision that permits a person to report an act of harassment, intimidation or bullying anonymously; however, this shall not be construed to permit formal disciplinary action solely on the basis of an anonymous report.

All acts of harassment, intimidation, or bullying shall be reported verbally to the school principal on the same day when the school employee or contracted service provider witnessed or received reliable information regarding any such incident. The principal shall inform the parents or guardians of all students involved in the alleged incident, and may discuss, as appropriate, the availability of counseling and other intervention services. All acts of harassment, intimidation, or bullying shall be reported in writing to the school principal within two school days of when the school employee or contracted service provider witnessed or received reliable information that a student had been subject to harassment, intimidation, or bullying;

(6) a procedure for prompt investigation of reports of violations and complaints, which procedure shall at a minimum provide that:

(a) the investigation shall be initiated by the principal or the principal's designee within one school day of the report of the incident and shall be conducted by a school anti-bullying specialist. The principal may appoint additional personnel who are not school anti-bullying specialists to assist in the investigation. The investigation shall be completed as soon as possible, but not later than 10 school days from the date of the written report of the incident of harassment, intimidation, or bullying. In the event that there is information relative to the investigation that is anticipated but not yet received by the end of the 10-day period, the school anti-bullying specialist may amend the original report of the results of the investigation to reflect the information;

(b) the results of the investigation shall be reported to the superintendent of schools within two school days of the completion of the investigation, and in accordance with regulations promulgated by the State Board of Education pursuant to the "Administrative Procedure Act," P.L.1968, c.410 (C.52:14B-1 et seq.), the superintendent may decide to provide intervention services, establish training programs to reduce harassment, intimidation, or bullying and enhance school climate, impose discipline, order counseling as a result of the findings of the investigation, or take or recommend other appropriate action;

(c) the results of each investigation shall be reported to the board of education no later than the date of the board of education meeting next following the completion of the investigation, along with information on any services provided, training established, discipline imposed, or other action taken or recommended by the superintendent;

(d) parents or guardians of the students who are parties to the investigation shall be entitled to receive information about the investigation, in accordance with federal and State law and regulation, including the nature of the investigation, whether the district found evidence of harassment, intimidation, or bullying, or whether discipline was imposed or services provided to address the incident of harassment, intimidation, or bullying. This information shall be provided in writing within 5 school days after the results of the investigation are reported to the board. A parent or guardian may request a hearing before the board after receiving the information, and the hearing shall be held within 10 days of the request. The board shall meet in executive session for the hearing to protect the confidentiality of the students. At the hearing the board may hear from the school anti-bullying specialist about the incident, recommendations for discipline or services, and any programs instituted to reduce such incidents;

(e) at the next board of education meeting following its receipt of the report, the board shall issue a decision, in writing, to affirm, reject, or modify the superintendent's decision. The board's decision may be appealed to the Commissioner of Education, in accordance with the procedures set forth in law and regulation, no later than 90 days after the issuance of the board's decision; and

(f) a parent, student, guardian, or organization may file a complaint with the Division on Civil Rights within 180 days of the occurrence of any incident of harassment, intimidation, or bullying based on membership in a protected group as enumerated in the "Law Against Discrimination," P.L.1945, c.169 (C.10:5-1 et seq.);

(7) the range of ways in which a school will respond once an incident of harassment, intimidation or bullying is identified, which shall be defined by the principal in conjunction with the school anti-bullying specialist, but shall include an appropriate combination of services that are available within the district such as counseling, support services, intervention services, and other programs, as defined by the commissioner. In the event that the necessary programs and services are not available within the district, the district may apply to the Department of Education for a grant from the "Bullying Prevention Fund" established pursuant to section 25 of P.L.2010, c.122 (C.18A:37-

28) to support the provision of out-of-district programs and services;

(8) a statement that prohibits reprisal or retaliation against any person who reports an act of harassment, intimidation or bullying and the consequence and appropriate remedial action for a person who engages in reprisal or retaliation;

(9) consequences and appropriate remedial action for a person found to have falsely accused another as a means of retaliation or as a means of harassment, intimidation or bullying;

(10) a statement of how the policy is to be publicized, including notice that the policy applies to participation in school-sponsored functions;

(11) a requirement that a link to the policy be prominently posted on the home page of the school district's website and distributed annually to parents and guardians who have children enrolled in a school in the school district; and

(12) a requirement that the name, school phone number, school address and school email address of the district anti-bullying coordinator be listed on the home page of the school district's website and that on the home page of each school's website the name, school phone number, school address and school email address of the school anti-bullying specialist and the district anti-bullying coordinator be listed. The information concerning the district anti-bullying coordinator and the

school anti-bullying specialists shall also be maintained on the department's website.[40]

The New Jersey law also (1) requires school districts to "annually establish, implement, document, and assess bullying prevention programs or approaches, and other initiatives involving school staff, students, administrators, volunteers, parents, law enforcement and community members";[41] (2) requires each principal in a school district to appoint an antibullying specialist who will lead all investigations and serve as a prevention specialist;[42] (3) requires each superintendent to appoint an antibullying coordinator who must collaborate with the antibullying specialists to assist in the prevention of and response to bullying;[43] (4) requires each school district to form a school safety team to foster and maintain a positive school environment by receiving and monitoring bullying reports, identifying patterns of bullying, and educating students and parents regarding bullying;[44] (5) requires newly hired teachers to complete a program on harassment, intimidation, and bullying;[45] (6) requires the state department of education to develop a guidance document for school districts to assist in the resolution of complaints;[46] (7) requires the state com-

---

40. N.J. Rev. Stat. § 18A:37-15.
41. *Id.* § 18A:37-17.
42. *Id.* § 18A:37-20.
43. *Id.*
44. *Id.* § 18A:37-21.
45. *Id.* § 18A:37-22.
46. *Id.* § 18A:37-24.

missioner of education to establish a protocol for the appeal or review of complaints that were not adequately addressed at the local level;[47] (8) requires the commissioner of education to establish workshops and training programs for the training of antibullying specialists and coordinators;[48] (9) requires the commissioner of education to develop an online tutorial on harassment, intimidation, and bullying;[49] (10) establishes a bullying prevention fund;[50] and (11) designates a week in October of each year as the "Week of Respect" to be observed by providing instruction regarding the prevention of harassment, intimidation, and bullying.[51]

Other states' laws vary in their stringency. The laws in Massachusetts, New Hampshire, Iowa, Florida, and Oregon have requirements that are also fairly extensive and provide for more than simply the adoption of an antibullying policy.[52] By contrast, Kansas, Georgia, and South Dakota do not require much more than the adoption of a policy.[53] The new South Dakota law includes a model bullying policy that school districts are required to follow until they adopt their own policy.[54]

---

47. *Id.* § 18A:37-25.

48. *Id.* § 18A:37-26.

49. *Id.* § 18A:37-27.

50. *Id.* § 18A:37-28.

51. *Id.* § 18A:37-29.

52. MASS. GEN. LAWS ANN. ch. 71, § 37O; N.H. REV. STAT. § 193-F:4; IOWA CODE § 280.28; FLA. STAT. ANN. § 1006.147; OR. REV. STAT. § 339.356.

53. KAN. STAT. ANN. § 72-8256; GA. CODE ANN. § 20-2-751.4; S.Bill No. 130 (S.D. 87th Sess. Legis. Assemb. 2012).

54. S. Bill No. 130, §§ 1, 6 (S.D. 87th Sess. Legis. Assemb. 2012).

Constitutional Issues

Antibullying measures involve a variety of constitutional issues. Although there are differing definitions of *bullying*, the common thread among all of them is a physical act or a communication in some form that has an adverse effect on a student. When the means of bullying are expressive in nature, the First Amendment is always a factor influencing the action that the government can take. Due to the private ownership of the technology used in cyberbullying, there are also Fourth Amendment issues that come into play. Finally, the due process clause guides both the drafting and the application of the content of bullying statutes and policies.

A. Freedom of Speech
1. Student Speech

The leading student free speech case is *Tinker v. Des Moines Independent Community School District*.[1] Pur-

---

1. Tinker v. Des Moines Indep. Cmty. Sch. Dist., 393 U.S. 503 (1969).

suant to a school policy, students were suspended for wearing black armbands in protest of the Vietnam War. The U.S. Supreme Court concluded that the policy violated the students' First Amendment rights. The Court stated thus: "First Amendment rights . . . are available to teachers and students. It can hardly be argued that either students or teachers shed their constitutional right to freedom of speech or expression at the schoolhouse gate."[2]

This case stands for the proposition that in order to be regulated, student speech must create, or be reasonably certain to create, a material or substantial disruption to the school's educational mission.[3] The Court emphasized that a school district must show more than a desire to avoid the discomfort and unpleasantness that accompany unpopular viewpoints.

The lower courts have yet to focus much attention on that portion of the Supreme Court's decision, which authorizes school officials to regulate the speech of students if that speech "involves . . . invasion of the rights of others."[4] Since cyberbullying frequently impacts the rights of others, it will be important to see whether the phrase *invasion of*

---

2. *Id.* at 506.

3. *See id.* at 514 ("[T]he record does not demonstrate any facts which might reasonably have led school authorities to forecast substantial disruption or material interference with school activities. . . .").

4. *See id.* at 513 (finding that "conduct by the student, in class or out of it, which for any reason—whether it stems from time, place, or type of behavior—materially disrupts classwork or involves substantial disorder or invasion of the rights of others is, of course, not immunized by the constitutional guarantee of freedom of speech").

the rights of others takes on heightened significance in the evolving jurisprudence in this area.

2. Lewd Speech

Not all student speech is protected, even if it occurs on school grounds. Although the courts have granted wide latitude to the content of speech in a public forum,[5] the same breadth of protection does not apply in school. *Bethel School District No. 403 v. Fraser*[6] is the lewd-speech case in which the U.S. Supreme Court upheld the suspension of a student who made a speech during a school-wide assembly that included elaborate, graphic, and explicit sexual metaphors. The Court found that schools have the responsibility of instilling in students "the habits and manners of civility" necessary to be productive citizens and that schools also have an interest in protecting younger students from sexually explicit speech.[7]

The Third Circuit, however, recently rejected an attempt by a school district to use *Fraser* as the basis for its punishment of a student who created a fake MySpace profile of his high school principal. In *Layshock v. Hermitage School District*,[8] the school district characterized the MySpace profile as "unquestionably vulgar, lewd and offen-

---

5. *See* Cohen v. California, 403 U.S. 15 (1971) (holding that wearing a jacket inside a court house with the "F" word printed on it was protected speech).
6. 478 U.S. 675 (1986).
7. *Id.* at 681.
8. 650 F.3d 205 (3d Cir. 2011).

sive" and therefore unprotected by the First Amendment when it ended up in the school community.[9] Although the Third Circuit had previously held that "a school may categorically prohibit lewd, vulgar or profane language,"[10] the court clarified its opinion and stated that this prohibition applied only when the speech occurred "inside Tinker's schoolhouse gate."[11] The court concluded that the student's speech never made it through the gate because it did not create any substantial disruption in school.

3. School-Sponsored Speech

When a school district creates a vehicle for student speech, the U.S. Supreme Court has recognized a right to control that speech. In *Hazelwood School District v. Kuhlmeier*,[12] the Supreme Court held that a high school newspaper published by students as part of a journalism class did not qualify as a public forum, which allowed school officials to retain the right to impose reasonable restrictions on student speech in the paper. The Court concluded that in determining when a school may refuse to lend its name and resources to the dissemination of student expression, "educators do not offend the First Amendment by exercising editorial control over the style and content of student speech in school-sponsored expressive activities so long as

---

9. *Id.* at 216.

10. *See* Saxe v. St. Coll. Area Sch. Dist., 240 F.3d 200, 214 (3d Cir. 2001).

11. *Hermitage Sch. Dist.*, 650 F.3d at 217 n.17.

12. 484 U.S. 260 (1988).

their actions are reasonably related to legitimate pedagogical concerns."[13] The Court noted a distinction between speech that happens to occur on school premises and that a school must tolerate and speech that a school affirmatively promotes.

4. Speech Advocating Drug Use

In *Morse v. Frederick*,[14] the U.S. Supreme Court once again had the opportunity to consider the reach of a school district in regulating the content of a student's speech. The *Morse* case involved a student who attended an Olympic Torch Relay event. Although the event was held off campus, it was a school-sponsored activity. The student refused to take down a banner reading "Bong Hits 4 Jesus" after he was instructed to do so by his principal. He was then suspended from school.

His suspension was upheld—because of the special nature of the school environment and the governmental interest in preventing student drug abuse—by a divided Supreme Court in a 5-4 decision empowering schools to restrict student expression that they "reasonably regard as promoting illegal drug use."[15]

Referring to the debate as to whether the Court in *Fraser* was regulating the content or the manner of Fraser's speech, Chief Justice Roberts said in his opinion for the majority:

13. *Id.* at 272–73.
14. 551 U.S. 393 (2007).
15. *Id.* at 408.

We need not resolve this debate to decide this case. For present purposes, it is enough to distill from *Fraser* two basic principles. First, *Fraser's* holding demonstrates that the constitutional rights of students in public school are not automatically coextensive with the rights of adults in other settings. Had Fraser delivered the same speech in a public forum outside the school context, it would have been protected. . . . Second, *Fraser* established that the mode of analysis set forth in *Tinker* is not absolute. Whatever approach *Fraser* employed, it certainly did not conduct the "substantial disruption" analysis prescribed by *Tinker*.[16]

In a separate concurring opinion in which Justice Kennedy joined, Justice Alito articulated the limited basis on which he concurred:

The opinion of the Court does not endorse the broad argument advanced by petitioners and the United States that the First Amendment permits public school officials to censor any student speech that interferes with a school's "educational mission." This argument can easily be manipulated in dangerous ways, and I would reject it before such abuse occurs. The "educational mission" of the public schools is defined by

---

16. *Id.* at 404–05.

the elected and appointed public officials with authority over the schools and by the school administrators and faculty. As a result, some public schools have defined their educational missions as including the inculcation of whatever political and social views are held by members of these groups.[17]

5. True Threats

In *Watts v. United States*,[18] the U.S. Supreme Court first recognized that threats of violence constituting "true threats" fall within those categories of speech that are not protected by the ambit of the First Amendment.[19] At a political debate during the Vietnam war, an eighteen-year-old man made the following statement about President Johnson: "[I]f they ever make me carry a rifle the first man I want in my sights is L.B.J." The Court stated that true threats are not protected by the First Amendment, but it ruled that the man's statement was not a true threat. The Court did not provide any test or guidance in determining what is a true threat. Instead, it simply said, "What is a threat must be distinguished from what is constitutionally protected speech."[20]

The very general guidance of the Supreme Court in *Watts* left ample room for the federal courts of appeals to devise more specific limits. The appellate courts have col-

17. *Id.* at 423 (Alito, Kennedy, JJ., concurring).
18. 394 U.S. 705 (1969).
19. *Id.*
20. *Id.* at 707.

lectively created an objective test that helps determine whether a statement is a true threat falling outside First Amendment protection. This test focuses on "whether a reasonable person would interpret the alleged threat as a serious expression of an intent to cause a present or future harm."[21] The views of the federal courts diverge, however, when trying to determine from whose viewpoint the statement should be determined—in other words, there is still a debate over whether this objective standard views the nature of the alleged threat from the perspective of a reasonable recipient or a reasonable speaker.[22]

The factors in each case that the courts may consider in determining whether an expression or speech is a true threat include the following: (1) the context in which the alleged threat was made, (2) the actions of the speaker and the reaction of those who heard the alleged threat, (3) whether the person who made the alleged threat communicated it directly to the object of the threat, (4) whether the speaker had a history of making threats against the person purportedly threatened, and (5) whether the recipient had a

---

21. United States v. Fulmer, 108 F.3d 1486, 1490–91 (1st Cir. 1990).

22. *Compare* Doe v. Pulaski County Special Sch. Dist., 306 F.3d 616, 622–23 (8th Cir. 2002) (viewing the alleged threat from the viewpoint of a reasonable recipient), *and* United States v. Malik, 16 F.3d 45, 49 (2d Cir. 1994), *cert. denied*, 513 U.S. 968, 130 L. Ed. 2d 347, 115 S. Ct. 435 (1994) (same), *and* United States v. Maisonet, 484 F.2d 1356, 1358 (4th Cir. 1973) (same), *with* United States v. Orozco-Santillan, 903 F.2d 1262, 1265 (9th Cir. 1990) (viewing the alleged threat from the speaker's viewpoint), *and* United States v. Welch, 745 F.2d 614, 620 (10th Cir. 1984) (same), *and* Mahaffey v. Aldrich, 236 F. Supp. 2d 779, 784 (E.D. Mich. 2002).

reason to believe that the speaker had a propensity to engage in violence.[23]

Two examples of the "true threat" analysis in the school context are found in *Doe v. Pulaski County Special School District*[24] and *Mardis v. Hannibal Public School District*.[25] In *Pulaski County*, a student wrote a letter threatening another student—his former girlfriend. The letter contained graphic language referring to the girlfriend in vile terms and stating a desire "to sodomize, rape, and kill" her. A friend of the young lady saw the letter, told the girl to whom it was addressed about its contents, and then gave the letter to her while she was at school. The U.S. Court of Appeals for the Eighth Circuit found that the letter contained a true threat and concluded that the student's expulsion did not violate the First Amendment. The court later used its ruling in *Pulaski County* as a basis, in part, for upholding the suspension in *Mardis* of a student who sent instant messages to a friend in which he identified students that he would "have to get rid of," including specific students as well as students who were "midget[s]," "fags," and "negro bitches." The student talked about using a .357 Magnum that he could borrow from a friend. The court found that the hate-filled comments coupled with the reference to a gun were sufficient for a reasonable person to perceive the comments as a true threat.

---

23. T.W. v. Sch. Dist. of Philadelphia, 2003 U.S. Dist. LEXIS 5945 (E.D. Pa. Apr. 8, 2003).
24. 306 F.3d 616 (8th Cir. 2002).
25. 647 F.3d 754 (8th Cir. 2011).

6. Fighting Words

In some instances, the U.S. Supreme Court has recognized that there is really no debate about the meaning of words or whether their use may be banned. In *Chaplinsky v. New Hampshire*,[26] the Supreme Court affirmed its long-standing position that "certain well-defined and narrowly limited classes of speech"—among them "the lewd and obscene, the profane, the libelous, and the insulting or 'fighting' words'"—may be prohibited and even punished by the government.[27] Subsequent cases have narrowed the *Chaplinsky* holding to only fighting words, i.e., words whose mere utterance entails a call to violence.[28]

7. Hate Speech

Recently, in *Snyder v. Phelps*,[29] the U.S. Supreme Court considered the protection afforded by the Constitution to hate speech. In that case, the father of a deceased military service member brought action against a fundamentalist church and its members, asserting that their antihomosexual protest at the funeral of the service member caused emotional distress. The Supreme Court ruled that the First Amendment was a defense to the action, stating thus: "Given that Westboro's speech was at a public place on a matter of public concern, that speech is entitled to 'special

---

26. 315 U.S. 568 (1942).

27. *Id.* at 573.

28. *See, e.g.*, Cohen v. California, 403 U.S. 15 (1971); Gooding v. Wilson, 405 U.S. 518 (1972).

29. 131 S. Ct. 1207 (2011).

protection' under the First Amendment. Such speech cannot be restricted simply because it is upsetting or arouses contempt."[30] Chief Justice Roberts concluded his majority opinion with these words:

> Speech is powerful. It can stir people to action, move them to tears of both joy and sorrow, and—as it did here—inflict great pain. On the facts before us, we cannot react to that pain by punishing the speaker. As a Nation we have chosen a different course—to protect even hurtful speech on public issues to ensure that we do not stifle public debate.[31]

In the setting of a secondary school, the antihomosexual epithets used by the speakers in *Snyder* do not enjoy the same protection, as evidenced by *Harper v. Poway Unified School District.*[32] In that case, a high school student in Poway, California, was ordered not to wear to school a T-shirt with "BE ASHAMED, OUR SCHOOL EMBRACED WHAT GOD HAS CONDEMNED" handwritten on the front and "HOMOSEXUALITY IS SHAMEFUL" handwritten on the back. He sought to do so in response to a "Day of Silence." The Day of Silence was promoted by the Gay-Straight Alliance at his school and approved by the school administration. The same administration prohibited him

---

30. *Id.* at 1219.
31. *Id.* at 1220.
32. 445 F.3d 1166 (2006).

from wearing the antihomosexual T-shirt because it was deemed to be inflammatory, in violation of the student dress code, and disruptive to the educational environment. The U.S. Court of Appeals for the Ninth Circuit found no violation of the student's rights because, it concluded, the free speech clause of the First Amendment permits public schools to restrict student speech that intrudes upon the rights of other students.

B. Fourth Amendment and Related Search Issues
1. Student Search Cases

The leading student search case is *New Jersey v. TLO*.[33] In *TLO*, the U.S. Supreme Court determined that searches of students by school officials implicate their constitutional rights against unlawful searches and seizures. The Court did not go so far as to require school officials to obtain a search warrant before conducting a search of a student, but it did require that searches of students must be reasonable under the circumstances.

The ruling of the Court is summarized in the following statement regarding the reasonableness requirement:

> Determining the reasonableness of any search involves a two-fold inquiry: first, one must consider "whether the . . . action was justified at its inception"; second, one must determine whether

---

33. 469 U.S. 325 (1985).

the search as actually conducted "was reasonably related in scope to the circumstances which justified the interference in the first place." Under ordinary circumstances, a search of a student by a teacher or other school official will be "justified at its inception" when there are reasonable grounds for suspecting that the search will turn up evidence that the student has violated or is violating either the law or the rules of the school. Such a search will be permissible in its scope when the measures adopted are reasonably related to the objectives of the search and not excessively intrusive in light of the age and sex of the student and the nature of the infraction.[34]

The principles of *TLO* have been revisited in the U.S. Supreme Court in two subsequent student cases, both involving drug testing: *Vernonia School District 47J v. Acton*[35] and *Board of Education of Pottawatomie County v. Earls.*[36] In *Vernonia*, the Supreme Court held that a school district's policy to randomly test students in athletic activities for drugs is allowable based on (1) the school's "custodial and tutelary" responsibility over children (the policy was adopted in furtherance of the government's responsibilities, under a public school system, as guardian and tutor of children entrusted to its care); (2) the dimin-

---

34. *Id.* at 341–42 (citations omitted).
35. 515 U.S. 646 (1995).
36. 536 U.S. 822 (2002).

ished expectation of privacy in athletic activities in light of the communal undress often present in locker rooms and the regulated nature of athletics; and (3) the nature and immediacy of the school's concern over the drastic increase in student drug use, particularly among athletes. In *Earls*, the Supreme Court concluded that a public high school's mandatory drug-testing program for all students involved in extracurricular activities was constitutional.

2. Computer and Electronic System Searches

Most of the relevant cases regarding computer or electronic system searches that are governed by the Fourth Amendment arise from employer-employee litigation. Although courts have generally given employers the benefit of the doubt, it is not clear whether school districts will receive the same treatment. However, given the diminished Fourth Amendment rights of students in the educational setting, it seems likely. In any event, to the extent that there is guidance, it is derived from cases in the employment arena.

The first electronic search case to make its way to the U.S. Supreme Court was *City of Ontario v. Quon*.[37] In *Quon*, the city sought to audit its usage plan for pagers assigned to employees, and it obtained transcripts of text messages from the wireless provider, which included redacted off-duty text messages. As a result of its audit, the city found that Quon had numerous non-work-related, often sexually explicit, texts, and so it disciplined him.

---

37. 130 S. Ct. 2619 (2010).

Quon challenged the city's action under the Fourth Amendment as an unreasonable search. The Supreme Court did not decide whether an employee had a "reasonable expectation of privacy in text messages."[38] The Court observed that technology is changing rapidly and so are society's expectations of proper behavior and privacy in communications. For purposes of its ruling, the Court assumed, without deciding, that the employee had a reasonable expectation of privacy but found that the search was reasonable anyway.

The Court held that the city had reasonable grounds for finding that an audit was necessary for a noninvestigatory, work-related purpose: the employer needed to know whether the wireless contract met the employer's needs. The search was reasonably related to the objectives of the search: determining whether the public employer was paying public monies for the personal communications of employees. And the search was not excessively intrusive—the city only requested a small sample of monthly text transcripts and redacted all off-duty texts. Therefore, the Court found no violation of the Fourth Amendment.

With regard to computers, federal courts have generally recognized the right of public employers to search their own computer systems; by extension, these principles should also apply to students as long as the electronic systems or devices are owned by the school itself. The case of *United States v. Angevine*[39] is an example of an employer's

---

38. *Id.* at 2630.
39. 281 F.3d 1130 (10th Cir. 2002).

search of its own computer system. In *Angevine*, the court held that an employee could not have an objectively reasonable expectation of privacy because reasonable university computer users should have been aware that network administrators and others were free to view data downloaded from the Internet. And in *Leventhal v. Knapek*,[40] even though an employee had some expectation of privacy in the contents of his workplace computer, the searches of the employee's computer that were conducted in this case were reasonable in light of the state employer's need to investigate the allegations of the employee's misconduct balanced against the modest intrusion caused by the searches.

3. Federal Laws

Electronic communications of students and all other users are protected and regulated by a number of federal laws: Omnibus Crime Control and Safe Streets Act of 1968 (Wiretap Act);[41] Stored Wire Communications Act;[42] Electronic Communications Privacy Act of 1986;[43] and Communications Decency Act.[44] These federal laws apply both to searches of electronic communications that are transmitted or stored by a school district's computer or telephone system and to electronic communications transmitted or stored on computers, cell phones, and electronic devices owned by students.

---

40. 266 F.3d 64 (2d Cir. 2001).
41. 18 U.S.C. §§ 2510–2525.
42. 18 U.S.C. §§ 2701 *et seq.*
43. 18 U.S.C. §§ 2510–3126.
44. 47 U.S.C. §§ 201 *et seq.*

Title III of the Wiretap Act prohibits the "interception" of covered wire and oral communications subject to two exemptions: (1) the prior consent exemption (an unambiguous consent by one party to a communication that a specific type of communication may be intercepted constitutes a consent to the interception of that type of communication) and (2) the service provider exemption (telephone companies and employers who provide wire communication services may monitor calls for service checks). An additional exemption has been recognized by the courts and is characterized as the business extension exemption (telephone extension equipment that is provided in the normal course of business may be used for ordinary business purposes to intercept business communications).

The prior consent exemption may have some application to electronic communication devices or systems owned by school districts. This exemption has been interpreted in a number of cases. In *Deal v. Spears*,[45] a liquor store owner began taping employee telephone calls after he told an employee that, due to excessive telephone usage, he might install a pay phone or monitor calls; the court determined that this notice was not sufficient to constitute consent. In *Watkins v. L.M. Berry & Co.*,[46] the court found that notice to employees that sales calls would be monitored was sufficient only for the monitoring of business calls and for the monitoring of personal calls to the extent necessary

---

45. 980 F.2d 1153 (8th Cir. 1992).
46. 704 F.2d 577 (11th Cir. 1983).

to determine that the call was not a business call. In *Griggs-Ryan v. Smith*,[47] the court ruled that if the employee gives prior consent and the consent is not limited, then consent will be implied for subsequent communications. And in *James v. Newspaper Agency Corp.*,[48] the U.S. Supreme Court found that monitoring was protected where the employer openly installed a monitoring system to give employees training and instruction on telephone techniques and notified all employees that monitoring would take place.

C. Due Process Issues
1. Procedural Due Process

The leading student procedural due process case is *Goss v. Lopez*.[49] In *Goss*, the U.S. Supreme Court determined that students have a property interest in their education and that public schools may not deprive them of this right without due process of law. The Court explained that even a short suspension of ten days or less from school would deprive a student of two protected interests: the student's "property interest," or entitlement to an education, and the student's "liberty interest" in his good name and reputation.[50]

After weighing and balancing considerations important to the school environment, the Court concluded that full-

---

47. 904 F.2d 112 (1st Cir. 1990).
48. 591 F.2d 579 (10th Cir. 1979).
49. 419 U.S. 565 (1975).
50. *Id.* at 576.

blown trials are not necessary when relatively short suspensions are at issue. Rather, in connection with a suspension of ten days or less, the student must be given (1) oral or written notice of the allegations against the student, (2) the basis in fact of the charges and an explanation of the evidence in support of the charge, and (3) the opportunity to respond to those charges.[51]

There is no requirement that the student be given time to prepare a response or that the student be given an opportunity to consult with counsel, or even a parent, before the student is allowed an opportunity to be heard. The Court observed that in the great majority of cases, the disciplinarian will informally discuss the alleged misconduct with the student, perhaps minutes after it occurred, and will give the student an opportunity to explain himself.

2. Vagueness Standard

As noted above, the vagueness standard applied by the courts to criminal statutes requires compliance with three essential principles, outlined in *State v. Nail:* (1) the statute must be clear enough so that people understand what conduct is prohibited, (2) the statute must be clear enough so that authority figures will not overstep their bounds and exercise their power arbitrarily or discriminatorily, and (3) the statute must not be so broad that constitutionally protected activities such as First Amendment speech become illegal.[52]

---

51. *Id.* at 581.
52. State v. Nail, 743 N.W.2d 535, 539 (Iowa 2007).

The criminal law standard regarding vagueness discussed in *Nail* is more restrictive than the standard typically applied by the courts to student discipline codes. For cases involving student discipline codes, courts are more likely to defer to the standard articulated in *Rose v. Locke*,[53] a case in which the U.S. Supreme Court reviewed a criminal statute alleged to be vague and therefore unconstitutional. The Court noted thus:

> It is settled that the fair-warning requirement embodied in the Due Process Clause prohibits the States from holding an individual "criminally responsible for conduct which he could not reasonably understand to be proscribed." But this prohibition against excessive vagueness does not invalidate every statute which a reviewing court believes could have been drafted with greater precision. Many statutes will have some inherent vagueness, for "[i]n most English words and phrases there lurk uncertainties." Even trained lawyers may find it necessary to consult legal dictionaries, treatises, and judicial opinions before they may say with any certainty what some statutes may compel or forbid. . . . All the Due Process Clause requires is that the law give sufficient warning that men may conduct themselves so as to avoid that which is forbidden.[54]

---

53. 423 U.S. 48 (1975).
54. *Id.* at 48, 49–50.

This less stringent standard was apparent in the *Fraser* case, in which the U.S. Supreme Court held that the rule providing that a student could be disciplined for disruptive conduct, which included "the use of obscene, profane language or gestures," was not void for vagueness.[55] The Court reflected the deference to which school officials are entitled in drafting student conduct codes: "Given the school's need to be able to impose disciplinary sanctions for a wide range of unanticipated conduct disruptive of the educational process, the school rules need not be as detailed as a criminal code which imposes criminal sanctions."[56]

Similarly, in the case of *Alex v. Allen*,[57] a federal district court held that the terms *flagrant disregard of teachers*, *loitering*, and *rowdy behavior* were not so vague as to violate constitutional standards. The court noted that although these terms might not meet the constitutional requirements of criminal statutes, "a looser standard of constitutional review of high school regulations is appropriate because of the greater flexibility possessed by the state to regulate the conduct of children as opposed to adults."[58]

---

55. Bethel Sch. Dist. No. 403 v. Fraser, 478 U.S. 675, 686 (1986).

56. *Id.*

57. 409 F. Supp. 379 (W.D. Pa. 1976).

58. *Id.* at 384.

Case Law

With the evolution of technology in communication and the expansion of its use by young people, the majority of bullying cases are now cases of cyberbullying.[1] President Obama noted the change in his remarks at the White House Conference on Bullying Prevention: "Today, bullying doesn't even end at the school bell—it can follow our children from the hallways to their cell phones to their computer screens."[2]

Courts have varied in their approach to the question of whether or not school districts may regulate bullying

---

1. *See generally* Kathleen Conn, *Cyberbullying and Other Student Technology Misuse in K-12 American Schools*, 16 WIDENER L. REV. 89 (2010); Thomas E. Wheeler, *Lessons from the Lord of the Flies: The Responsibility of Schools to Protect Students from Internet Threats and Cyber-Hate Speech*, 215 EDUC. L. REP. 227 (2007); Sarah O'Cronan, *Grounding Cyberspeech: Public Schools' Authority to Discipline Students for Internet Activity*, 97 KY. L.J. 149 (2008–2009).

2. President Obama and the First Lady at the White House Conference on Bullying Prevention, WHITEHOUSE.GOV (Mar. 10, 2011), *available at* http://www.whitehouse.gov/photos-and-video/video/2011/03/10/president-obama-first-lady-conference-bullying-prevention#transcript.

that occurs after the school bell rings. This portion of the monograph will review the case law that has developed regarding the right of a school district to regulate cyberbullying that occurs off campus.[3]

A. Cases Rejecting the District's Right to Regulate
1. *Mahaffey v. Aldrich*

In *Mahaffey v. Aldrich*,[4] a school district suspended a student, Mahaffey, from school after the school learned of a website that the student had created entitled "Satan's web page." The website created a mission for readers: "SATAN'S MISSION FOR YOU THIS WEEK: Stab someone for no reason then set them on fire throw them off a cliff, watch them suffer and with their last breath, just before everything goes black, spit on their face." The website also listed "people I wish would die." According to the student, the website was created "just for laughs," and he did not think that anyone else would end up seeing it. As a disclaimer, the website stated, "PLEASE DON'T GO KILLING PEOPLE AND STUFF THEN BLAMING IT ON ME." A parent of one of the students at Mahaffey's school noticed the website and noti-

---

3. A majority of the following cases are decisions rendered at the trial or district court level. For a collection of lower court case decisions protecting student speech, see also Philip T.K. Daniel & Scott Greytak, *A Need to Sharpen the First Amendment Countours of Off-Campus Student Speech*, 273 EDUC. L. REP. 21, 32 (2011).

4. 236 F. Supp. 2d 779 (E.D. Mich. 2002).

fied the police. The police subsequently notified the school. Mahaffey was suspended.

Utilizing *Tinker v. Des Moines Independent Community School District*,[5] the court held that the school could only punish the student for his speech on the website if that speech "'substantially interfere[d] with the work of the school or impinge[d] upon the rights of other students.'"[6] Applying this standard to the facts of the case, the court found that the student did not communicate the statements on the website to anyone and that there was no evidence in the record to prove there was any disruption to the school or campus activity as a result of the creation of the website. It was unclear whether the student had used any school property to work on the website; he said that he "may have" used school computers. Therefore, the court ruled that the school's actions against the student violated his First Amendment rights.

The court also found that the student's due process rights were violated by the school's actions in disciplining him. The hearing that the student was afforded to protest his suspension was not accompanied by proper notice. Notice of the decision made at the hearing was sent to the student more than a month after the hearing had already taken place. Additionally, the student was not allowed to cross-examine witnesses at his hearing.

---

5. 393 U.S. 503 (1969).

6. *Mahaffey*, 236 F. Supp. 2d at 784 (quoting *Tinker*, 393 U.S. at 509).

2. *Beussink v. Woodland R-IV School District*

In *Beussink v. Woodland R-IV School District*,[7] a high school student, Beussink, posted on the Internet a personal website that he had created on his home computer outside of school hours. The website used vulgar language to criticize the school administration and invited others to share their opinion of the administration. A hyperlink to the school's official website was provided on the student's web page.

Another student, angry with Beussink at the time, accessed the site at the school and showed it to a teacher. The teacher testified that she was upset by what she read on the website, and she proceeded to go directly to the principal with the information. Beussink had not asked the student to access the website, nor did he provide her with the website address. Instead, the student had seen the website when she used Beussink's computer at his house.

After reviewing the website, the principal testified that he decided to discipline Beussink even though he did not conduct an investigation to determine if any other students had seen or had knowledge of the site. Several witnesses for the school district testified that although the student's website was accessed, it did not cause a disruption in the school. The first disciplinary action was issued to Beussink while he was in his fourth-period class. It was a five-day sus-

---

7. 30 F. Supp. 2d 1175 (E.D. Mo. 1998).

pension. Later that day, the principal rethought the five-day suspension and increased it to ten days.

The student filed suit against the school district alleging that the principal's disciplinary action against him violated his free speech rights. The court found that the principal's action constituted an impermissible attempt to regulate speech based solely on its content. The court found no evidence that the student's website created a reasonable fear that it would materially or substantially interfere with school discipline. Rather, the court stated that the principal was upset by the website. Although there was some disruption because of the website, it did not rise to the level of material or substantial disruption that is necessary to allow for regulation. The court found that, in the absence of a finding that the speech substantially interfered with school discipline, the school was not permitted to limit or censor such speech simply because it was unpopular.

3. *Beidler v. North Thurston School District No. 3*

In *Beidler v. North Thurston School District No. 3*,[8] a high school student was expelled after the school became aware of a satirical website that the student created and was maintaining on his home computer. The site parodied one of the school's assistant principals, showing him having sexual relations with a cartoon character.

---

8. No. 99-00236 (Wash. Super. Ct. July 18, 2000) (unreported).

The court in this case found that the school could not discipline the student for his out-of-school speech because the evidence did not show material and substantial disruption of the work or discipline of the school. Although the court conceded that the student's words may very well have defamed the assistant principal, the court held that the First Amendment does not permit the school district to justify its discipline of students engaged in otherwise protected speech because the content defames a person whose interests are identical to the interests of the school district.

4. *Killion v. Franklin Regional School District*

In *Killion v. Franklin Regional School District*,[9] a member of the track team created a "Top Ten" list about the school's athletic director, calling him fat, attacking his masculinity, and mocking the size of his genitals. The list was compiled on the student's computer at his home and was sent to some friends via e-mail. The student never distributed the list either electronically or in print at school, but the list nevertheless made its way onto school grounds. When confronted about the list, the student admitted responsibility for creating it. The student was suspended for creating the list because it contained offensive remarks about a school official, it was found on school grounds, and he admitted to its creation.

The court ruled that the school district violated the student's free speech rights by disciplining him for speech

---

9. 136 F. Supp. 2d 446 (W.D. Pa. 2001).

when there was no evidence that the speech actually disrupted or was likely to disrupt the school's educational mission. No evidence was presented demonstrating that the teachers were unable to teach because of the list. Additionally, the list had been on school grounds for several days prior to the administration discovering its existence. Finally, one week passed after the administration found out before it took any disciplinary action. The school offered justification based on the student's prior history and the possible threat of disruption: he had created and brought similar lists to the school in the past and had been told not to do so. However, the court stated that there was no evidence of a substantial disruption stemming from the student's past behavior, so there was no viable threat of disruption present. The court also said that antics such as those present in this case cannot, without more, impair a teacher's ability to teach.

In addition, the court stated that, in the absence of exceptional circumstances, the school could not discipline a student for lewd, vulgar, or profane speech that occurs off school grounds and found that its attempt to do so was constitutionally overbroad: "Given the out of school creation of the list, absent evidence that Paul was responsible for bringing the list on school grounds, and absent disruption . . . we hold . . . that defendants could not, without violating the First Amendment, suspend Paul for the mere creation of the Bozutto Top Ten list."[10] The court found that the school's policy was overbroad because there were no geo-

---

10. *Id.* at 458.

graphical limitations in the policy, and it was not limited to substantial disruption or interference of school operations. Finally, the court stated that the policy was void for vagueness because there was no definition of *abuse* present. The rule was devoid of any detail that would inform a student of the nature of prohibited conduct.

5. *Emmett v. Kent School District*

In *Emmett v. Kent School District,* a high school student created a website from his home "without using school resources or time."[11] The web page was entitled "Unofficial Kentlake High Home Page," and there was a disclaimer that it was not sponsored by the school. The web page included mock obituaries, and visitors to the site were invited to vote to decide who would die next. The mock obituaries stemmed from an English class assignment and were a joke among the students. However, the website was sensationalized in the local press, and the student was initially placed on emergency expulsion for intimidation, harassment, disruption to the educational process, and violation of the school's copyright. This punishment was later modified to a five-day suspension.

The court found a violation of the student's free speech rights based on the school district's punishment of him for the content of his personal website. There was no evidence that the website was intended to threaten or did threaten

---

11. 92 F. Supp. 2d 1088, 1089 (W.D. Wash. 2000).

others or that it manifested violent tendencies in the student. The court stated, "Although the intended audience was undoubtedly connected to Kentlake High School, the speech was entirely outside of the school's supervision or control."[12]

6. *Coy v. Board of Education of North Canton City Schools*

In *Coy v. Board of Education of North Canton City Schools*,[13] a high school student, Coy, created a website on his home computer outside of school hours that included pictures of three middle school students with insulting statements written under each of the pictures. The section was entitled "losers." Although there were insulting sentences about each boy, there was no obscene material posted. One boy was described as being sexually aroused by his mother. Coy was at first suspended for four days. This punishment was subsequently increased to an eighty-day expulsion.

The student and his parents challenged the disciplinary action as a violation of the student's First Amendment rights. Although the website was accessed on school grounds, it was created at the student's home. Since he did not try to show the web page to other students at school, there was no disruption created at school. The information

---

12. *Id.* at 1090.
13. 205 F. Supp. 791 (N.D. Ohio 2002).

on the website was crude, but it was not sexually explicit like the speech in *Bethel School District No. 403 v. Fraser.*[14] The student also asserted that one or more of the applicable disciplinary policies were unconstitutionally overbroad and vague.

The court found that all three of the rules under which the student was disciplined could reach a substantial amount of protected speech, so the school district's motion for summary judgment on those claims was not granted. The court then denied the school district's motion for summary judgment on two of the student's claims and sustained the student's motion for summary judgment on the claim that one of the policies (a catchall provision) was impermissibly vague because there was no indication of what actions or behavior could lead to disciplinary action from the school. Finally, the court ruled that there was no evidence that there was a chilling of First Amendment rights, and it rejected that claim.

7. *Flaherty v. Keystone Oaks School District*

In *Flaherty v. Keystone Oaks School District,*[15] a high school student posted four messages on a website message board, three from his parents' home computer and one from school. The messages pertained to an upcoming volleyball game with a rival school, and in the messages the student criticized or mocked the opposing team and a

---

14. 478 U.S. 675 (1986).
15. 247 F. Supp. 2d 698 (W.D. Pa. 2003).

teacher from the rival school. The student was disciplined for his communications and sued the school district asserting that the policies under which he was disciplined were unconstitutionally vague and overbroad.

The school attempted to shift the court's attention away from the handbook (under which they disciplined the student) and focus it toward the board policies to demonstrate that students still enjoyed freedom of expression. However, the court focused on the handbook, noting that it did not link the discipline to any substantial disruption and lacked any geographical limitation; therefore, it was unconstitutionally overbroad. The court also held that the rules were vague. No definitions were provided for words such as *offend, abuse, harassment,* or *inappropriate.* There was no way for a student to know what would violate the rule and lead to discipline. Because the rules were both vague and overboard, the court declined to enforce them and overturned the disciplinary action taken against the student.

8. *Layshock v. Hermitage School District*

In *Layshock v. Hermitage School District,*[16] Layshock, a senior student, used a computer at his grandmother's home

---

16. 650 F.3d 205 (3d Cir. 2011). The *Hermitage School District* case and *Blue Mountain School District* cases were decided on the same day in the Third Circuit. The two appellate panels reached opposite conclusions in their opinions, and both decisions were vacated and scheduled for rehearing en banc. The subsequent opinions were both released on June 13, 2011.

during nonschool hours and created a parody of the high school principal on Myspace.com. The website included a photograph of the principal, and the parody depicted the principal as gay and as a drunk. It also contained allegations that he was a steroid user, used a number of other drugs, and was transgender. The student entered the school district's website to obtain the photo that he used. The student admitted to the administration that he had created the page. He was then punished with a ten-day suspension, placed in the alternative education program, banned from all extracurricular activities, and prohibited from participating in graduation.

Layshock filed suit contending that the district's policies were overly broad and vague and that his punishment constituted a violation of his First Amendment rights and his Fourteenth Amendment right to due process. The court granted summary judgment to the student on his First Amendment claim but denied summary judgment to his parents on their substantive due process claim. The court found that there was not a sufficient nexus between the parody web page and the school district to establish foreseeable and substantial disruption of the school. Since the website was not created on school grounds and did not result in disruption of school operations, any punishment of the student for creating the web page would be reaching too far outside the schoolhouse gates.

At the rehearing, the school district conceded that Layshock's speech did not substantially disrupt the school environment. Instead, the district argued that there was no need for proof of substantial disruption because the speech was lewd and the district could punish it for that reason. As a result, the court did not decide whether *Tinker* is applicable to off-grounds conduct. Instead, the court decided that Layshock's copying of the principal's photograph from the school district's website did not constitute entering the school and that the school district was not empowered to punish this out-of-school conduct.

The concurring opinion directly addressed the issue of the applicability of *Tinker* to off-campus expressive conduct. The two concurring judges noted that the issue was one of "high importance," and they concluded that *Tinker* did apply to off-campus speech. The concurrence noted the elusive limitation that flows from the demarcation of a property line, and the judges wisely observed thus:

> With the tools of modern technology, a student could, with malice aforethought, engineer egregiously disruptive events and, if the trouble-maker were savvy enough to tweet the organizing communications from his or her cellphone while standing one foot outside the school property, the school administrators might succeed in heading off the actual disruption in the building but would be left powerless to discipline the student.[17]

---

17. *Id.* at 220–21 (Jordan, Vanaskie, JJ., concurring).

Since there was no showing of disruption in this case, the concurring judges stated that they would apply *Tinker* but reach the same ultimate conclusion.

9. *J.S. v. Blue Mountain School District*

In *J.S. v. Blue Mountain School District*,[18] J.S. and a fellow middle school student created a fake MySpace profile for their principal, identifying him as a bisexual and a pedophile. They also made derogatory statements about his wife and child. The picture for the page was acquired from the school's website. There was no indication that J.S. and her classmate actually believed their allegations to be true. Many students at the school viewed the fake profile, and some of them eventually told the principal. Because the students were not able to access the page while actually at the school, it had to be viewed at an off-campus location. The principal suspended J.S. and the other student for ten days.

J.S. then sued the district, claiming that her First Amendment rights were violated by the two-week suspension because the profile was nonthreatening and nonobscene and a parody. The disruption that resulted consisted of teachers having to quiet their classes twice, two students decorating J.S.'s locker when she returned from suspension, and a general lack of discipline among the eighth graders after the two students were disciplined. The court determined that there was no substantial and material disruption of school operations resulting from the profile cre-

---

18. 650 F.3d 915 (3d Cir. 2011). See comment at *supra* note 16.

ated at home, either actually occurring or reasonably forecasted to occur, because the profile was so outrageous that no one could have taken it seriously.

With respect to the district court's finding that the school district acted properly when it disciplined J.S. because the lewd and vulgar off-campus speech had an effect on campus, the court at the rehearing rejected the argument that *Fraser* legitimizes the disciplinary action because the student's speech was lewd. This argument failed because the court determined that *Fraser* could only be used to regulate in-school conduct, not out-of-school conduct. The court found that to apply the *Fraser* standard on the facts of this case would allow the school officials to "punish any speech by a student that takes place anywhere, at any time, as long as it is *about* the school or a school official, and is deemed 'offensive' by the prevailing authority."[19] In harmony with its decision in *Hermitage School District*, the court decided in favor of J.S. on her free speech claim.

The parents also made a Fourteenth Amendment claim with regard to their liberty interest in disciplining their own child. The court granted summary judgment on this claim in favor of the school district because the parents' ability to discipline was not disrupted by the school's actions.

Finally, the court rejected J.S.'s claim that the disciplinary rules under which she was punished were unconstitutionally vague and overbroad. The rules were limited to conduct that occurred at school. As written, the court

---

19. 650 F.3d at 933 (emphasis in original).

found that the rules were not vague. The challenge brought by J.S. pertained to the interpretation of the rules, not their content, and that challenge failed.

The concurrence in this case stated that *Tinker* should never be applied to off-grounds speech because it could be argued that a substantial disruption was caused by almost any kind of speech, even the most protected. Six judges dissented and stated their belief that *Tinker* should be used to govern the conduct. The dissenters concentrated on the lewdness of the speech, the fact that a school official was the target of the speech, and the fact that the photograph used on the website had been obtained from the school district's website. The dissent argued that these three factors created a reasonably foreseeable threat of a material and substantial disruption.

10. *J.C. v. Beverly Hills Unified School District*

In *J.C. v. Beverly Hills Unified School District*,[20] a high school student used her home computer to create a YouTube video. The video referred to another student as "spoiled," a "slut," and "the ugliest piece of sh— I've ever seen in my whole life." Again from her home, the student posted the video to the Internet and told the victim and other students about the video. The student about whom the video was made was very upset, and she and her mother brought it to the attention of school officials the next day. School district administrators then accessed the video on

---

20. 711 F. Supp. 2d 1094 (C.D. Cal. 2010).

school grounds, which was the only time that it was viewed on campus.

The student was suspended for two days and sued for violation of her First Amendment rights. In order for the school to establish substantial disruption, the court said, there needed to be more than students simply talking about the incident. There must be some actual disruption to the learning environment. In reality, the administrators were punishing the student for forcing them to do their job (dealing with upset parents and counseling their students). Additionally, the fear that students gossiped and passed notes in class about the issue was not the equivalent of a real risk of future substantial disruption. Likewise, the fear that violence would break out over the video was far too speculative in this case. The court found a violation of the First Amendment and stated, "This Court does not wish to see school administrators become censors of students' speech at all times, in all places, and under all circumstances. . . . Such broad authority would clearly intrude upon the rights of parents to 'direct the rearing of their children.'"[21] For all of these reasons, the court found a violation of the student's constitutional rights.

11. *Evans v. Bayer*

In *Evans v. Bayer*,[22] a high school student created a group on Facebook entitled "Ms. Sarah Phelps is the worst teacher I've ever met." The group's purpose was for stu-

---

21. *Id.* at 1110 n.8 (citations omitted).
22. 684 F. Supp. 2d 1365 (S.D. Fla. 2010).

dents to express their dislike for Ms. Phelps, a teacher. The page included the teacher's photograph. The posting, which did not contain threats of violence, was made after school hours from the student's home computer. The teacher never saw the posting, and it did not disrupt school activities. The student removed the posting after two days.

After its removal, the posting came to the attention of the principal. The student was suspended by the principal for three days and forced to move from her Advanced Placement classes into lesser-weighted honors courses. The student sued for violation of her First and Fourteenth Amendment rights.

The court found that the student's creation of the group constituted off-campus speech that was protected by the First Amendment. It was an opinion of a student about a teacher that was published off campus; did not cause any disruption on campus; was not lewd, vulgar, or threatening; and did not advocate illegal or dangerous behavior. The court did note that student off-campus speech, though generally protected, could be subject to analysis under the material/substantial disruption standard in *Tinker* to the extent that the speech raised on-campus concerns. However, the court explained that the student's speech in this case was never accessed on campus and did not create an expectation of substantial disruption, and the fact that it was aimed at a particular audience at the school was not enough by itself to label the speech as on-campus speech. The court noted, however, that certain classes of speech are not granted constitutional protection (i.e., fighting words).

B. Cases Upholding the District's Right to Regulate

1. *J.S. v. Bethlehem Area School District*

In *J.S. v. Bethlehem Area School District*,[23] J.S., an eighth grade student, created a website at home using his own computer that posted "derogatory, profane, offensive and threatening comments" about his algebra teacher and the school's principal. On one web page, J.S. posted a request for donations to help pay a hit man to kill his algebra teacher. He also included a video that compared the teacher to Hitler.

These threats led to a serious disruption of the educational process because the teacher at whom most of the threats were directed experienced serious mental stress and anxiety, requiring her to take medical leave for the following school year, and the school had to hire three different substitute teachers to finish out the year and cover her classes. In addition, the entire school community suffered from the aftershocks of the circulation of this website: the effect on the school's community was described as akin to the death of a student.

The school took no immediate action against J.S. other than to ask him to remove the site, and he did so. No referral for psychological evaluation was made. At the end of the school year, the district sent a letter to J.S. and his parents suspending him because of the incident; after a hearing, the district decided to begin expulsion proceedings against J.S.

---

23. 807 A.2d 847 (Pa. 2002).

His family moved him to an out-of-state school, so J.S. was unable to attend the expulsion hearing at which the district voted to expel him. J.S. appealed his case, and it eventually reached the Pennsylvania Supreme Court.

After considering the totality of the evidence, the court concluded that the website and its content did not contain "true threats." The court considered the website to be a "crude, highly offensive and perhaps misguided attempt at humor or parody . . . [but] did not reflect a serious . . . intent to inflict harm."[24] Furthermore, the district's failure to take immediate action undermined its argument that J.S. posed a true threat.

However, the court found that although the website had been created off school grounds, it had been accessed at school by J.S. and was aimed at the specific school and/or its personnel and should therefore be considered on-campus speech. In light of the significant adverse impact on the school community, the court found that the district had shown that the website created an "actual and substantial interference with the work of the school" so as to satisfy *Tinker*. As such, J.S.'s expulsion was not a violation of his First Amendment rights.

2. *Wisniewski v. Board of Education of Weedsport Central School District*

In *Wisniewski v. Board of Education of Weedsport Central School District*,[25] Wisniewski's instant messenger icon

---

24. *Id.* at 859.
25. 494 F.3d 34 (2d Cir. 2007), *cert. denied*, 128 S. Ct. 1741 (2008).

on his home computer featured the image of a gun shooting a person in the head and bearing the caption "Kill Mr. VanderMolen," Wisniewski's high school English teacher. The icon was shared with approximately fifteen of Wisniewski's classmates via chats on instant messenger. The school board suspended Wisniewski for a semester for making a threat on the Internet to kill one of his teachers.

Wisniewski appealed this decision, claiming that it violated his First Amendment rights. Based on the context, the court dismissed Wisniewski's First Amendment claims, finding that (1) intent or ability to carry out a threat is not relevant; (2) although the conduct took place off school grounds, the threat was directed at a teacher at the school, and the icon was circulated among Wisniewski's classmates for three weeks; and (3) the icon caused a substantial disturbance at the school. The court also stated that, in this case, it was reasonably foreseeable that the conduct would come to the attention of the authorities and that the effect would be a substantial disruption to the work and discipline of the school.

3. *Doninger v. Niehoff*

In *Doninger v. Niehoff*,[26] a student who was a class officer posted multiple messages on her publicly accessible blog in which she criticized the decisions of school administrators relating to a music program called Jamfest. In her blog, she told readers that "jamfest is cancelled due to douchebags in central office." In a later message, she copied into her blog

---

26. 527 F.3d 41 (2d Cir. 2008).

a letter of concern that her mother had sent to the school and suggested that it could be used "to get an idea of what to write if you want to write something or call to piss her off." The "her" referred to in the blog posting was the superintendent. The administration was upset because, among other things, the blog posts contained false information about the event: the school had not yet canceled the event but instead had agreed to move it to another date.

School district administrators disciplined the student by denying her the opportunity to run for a senior class officer position. The court rejected the student's First Amendment claims, finding that it was reasonably foreseeable that her speech would reach school property and have disruptive consequences because (1) the blog post directly pertained to an event at school, (2) the post invited students to read and respond to it, (3) students did in fact respond to the post, and (4) administrators became aware of the post. Additionally, the ability to run for student government is a privilege, not a right, so the student was not deprived of an interest entitled to constitutional protection.

4. *Kowalski v. Berkeley County Schools*

In *Kowalski v. Berkeley County Schools*,[27] a student created and posted to a MySpace web page called "S.A.S.H.," which the student claimed stood for "Students Against Sluts Herpes." The student claimed that she wanted to make other students actively aware of sexually transmitted dis-

---

27. 652 F.3d 565 (4th Cir. 2011).

eases. The student created the discussion group web page at home. After creating the group, the student invited approximately one hundred people on her "friends" list to join the group; approximately two dozen students responded and joined. The page was accessed first by another student at school during an after-hours class. It was reported that *S.A.S.H.* was an acronym for "Students Against Shay's Herpes," referring to the student who was the main subject of discussion on the web page. The page was "largely dedicated to ridiculing" that student.[28]

The school received a complaint of harassment from the target student's parents, and the target student was forced to miss school to avoid further abuse. School administrators suspended the student who created the web page for five days and issued her a ninety-day social suspension.

The student alleged, among other claims, violation of her rights under the First and Fourteenth Amendments. The court concluded that the school district's imposition of the sanction was permissible, explaining that the student used the Internet to orchestrate a targeted attack on a classmate and did so in manner that was sufficiently connected to the school environment as to implicate the school district's recognized authority to discipline speech that materially and substantially interferes with the requirements of appropriate discipline in the operation of the school and collides with the rights of others. The court also rejected

---

28. *Id.* at 565.

the student's procedural due process claim that she was not put on notice that she could be subjected to discipline for behavior outside of school, finding that the school's prohibitions on bullying and harassment were designed to regulate student behavior that affected the school's learning environment.

5. *Mardis v. Hannibal Public School District*

In *Mardis v. Hannibal Public School District*,[29] a student was chatting via instant message on his computer with a classmate. During the course of their conversation, the student told the classmate that he was going to get a gun and kill certain other classmates. The school district suspended the student for the remainder of the school year for his threatening communications, and the student sued the school district.

The court rejected the student's free speech claims, finding that the instant messages constituted student speech because, although the communications occurred off school grounds, the communications were made to a classmate who immediately forwarded the messages to school administrators, and the message disrupted the school community instantaneously. The court also found that the messages were true threats not protected by the First Amendment and were cause for substantial disruption in the school due to parent and student reactions/complaints to the threats and increased security measures.

---

29. 684 F. Supp. 2d 1114 (E.D. Miss. 2010).

In *D.J.M. v. Hannibal Public School District #60*,[30] the appellate court affirmed the district court's decision.

C. Summary and Analysis

When the U.S. Supreme Court denied certiorari in the *Blue Mountain School District* and *Hermitage School District* cases, school districts, educators, students, and parents lost their best opportunity to receive guidance from the high court that could settle some critical issues regarding student speech in cyberspace and provide consistency throughout the country. What we are left with today is a series of unanswered questions. What follows is my assessment of the likely answers to a few of those questions.

1. Do the Principles of *Tinker* Apply to the Off-Campus Conduct of Students?

I think that most courts would not apply *Tinker* unless there was evidence that the conduct actually caused some disruption in the school or was likely to cause some disruption. Schools generally do not have the right to regulate any off-campus conduct of students unless that conduct affects the operation of the school. Thus, schools that wish to do so will have the burden of persuading the court that there is a connection to the school. To paraphrase Jerry Maguire, the courts thus far are saying, "Show me the nexus!"

---

30. 647 F.3d 754 (8th Cir. 2011).

2. What Proof Will Be Required in Order to Apply *Tinker* to Off-Campus Conduct?

Proof of nexus seems to require evidence of actual disruption or at least evidence that disruption is likely to occur. Courts are not persuaded by evidence that students are merely talking about the conduct or speech that the school seeks to punish. This is uncomfortably close to the heckler's veto. In addition, unless the disruption is very serious, the courts are likely to require evidence that the disruption occurred for more than a brief period of time.

These are some of the factors that I think the courts would consider in making this decision: (1) the number of incidents of disruption that were reported; (2) the nature and severity of those incidents; (3) the number of students involved in those incidents; (4) the number of students affected by those incidents; (5) the physical and emotional impact of the incidents on students; (6) the number of school personnel affected by those incidents (teachers whose classes were disrupted, administrators who were required to answer calls and e-mails, personnel who were required to investigate and respond, etc.); (7) the amount of time spent by principals, counselors, nurses, etc., addressing the incidents and taking some action; (8) the number of school days during which the incidents occurred; (9) whether the student used any school resources in the communication or conduct (computer system, photocopier, physical or electronic bulletin board, etc.); (10) whether the student knew or should have known that the off-campus communication or conduct would be disseminated or communicated on campus; and (11) if there have been no actual incidents, then the factual basis for the forecast by administrators that disruption is likely to occur.

3. Do the Principles of *Fraser* Apply to the Off-Campus Conduct of Students?

Because the decision in *Fraser* was based on the content of the student's speech and because the U.S. Supreme Court in *Morse v. Frederick*[31] said that Fraser's speech would have been protected if it had been delivered in a public forum outside of school, I think that the courts will be reluctant to apply the "lewd or vulgar" standard to off-campus speech or conduct. The Third Circuit was invited to do so in *Blue Mountain School District* and declined. The natural disinclination of courts to engage in what will be viewed as censorship will likely be enough to discourage them from using *Fraser* to punish students for what they have said or done outside of school.

4. When, If Ever, Does Speech or Conduct That Is Clearly Off-Campus in Nature Become On-Campus and Subject to Regulation by the School?

This is generally a nexus question and is subject to the assessment of the factors identified in answer to Question #2. (See, for example, *Bethlehem Area School District*, in which the court stated, "We find there is a sufficient nexus

---

31. 551 U.S. 393 (2007).

between the website and the school campus to consider the speech as occurring on-campus.")[32]

However, the rapid expansion of technology-based communication devices and systems has caused a blurring of the boundary line between the campus and areas that are off campus, and this seems to influence courts in their determination of whether the required nexus exists. In fact, at least one court (the federal district court in *Beverly Hills Unified School District*) has stated that the majority rule is that "[t]he geographic origin of the speech is not material; *Tinker* applies to both on-campus and off-campus speech."[33]

5. Will the Courts Adopt a Broader Standard for Regulation of Student Conduct Based on the "Invasion of the Rights of Others" Principle Enunciated in *Tinker*?

The U.S. Supreme Court's ruling in *Tinker* has most often been characterized as permitting school districts to regulate student speech if there is a showing of actual or foreseeable substantial disruption; but when courts use a substantial disruption standard in student speech cases, they are misreading *Tinker*. What the Court actually said was as follows:

---

32. J.S. v. Bethlehem Area Sch. Dist., 807 A.2d 847, 865 (Pa. 2002).

33. J.C. v. Beverly Hills Unified Sch. Dist., 711 F. Supp. 2d 1094, 1108 (C.D. Cal. 2010).

But conduct by the student, in class or out of it,
which for any reason—whether it stems from time,
place, or type of behavior—materially disrupts
classwork or involves substantial disorder or invasion of the rights of others is, of course, not immunized by the constitutional guarantee of freedom of
speech.[34]

To the extent that a court uses a substantial disruption
standard, it does so only by merging two separate standards: material disruption of classwork and substantial disorder. There is no Supreme Court authority for such a
merged standard. Instead, there are three separate standards for the regulation of student speech, and all three are
authorized under *Tinker*: student speech may be regulated
if it materially disrupts classwork or involves substantial
disorder or involves invasions of the rights of others. Although attention has not yet been focused on the third standard (invasion of the rights of others), the time is certainly
ripe for advocacy groups to direct the attention of the
courts to this standard because it would dramatically
change the judicial discourse concerning bullying that is
based on speech.

---

34. Tinker v. Des Moines Indep. Cmty. Sch. Dist., 393 U.S. 503, 512
(1969).

Federal Guidance on Harassment

The limited nature of federal guidance on harassment is evident in the following statement from *Peer-to-Peer Violence and Bullying: Examining the Federal Response*, the 2011 U.S. Commission on Civil Rights annual report. In 2011, the Commission decided to devote its report to bullying, and in that report the Commission stated: "Federal civil rights laws—and the federal government's enforcement of those laws—are limited to heightened incidents of harassment that do not include typical schoolyard bullying unless that bullying creates a hostile environment."[1] What is most notable at the federal level is the absence of statutes and enforceable

---

1. U.S. COMM'N ON CIVIL RIGHTS, PEER-TO-PEER VIOLENCE AND BULLYING: EXAMINING THE FEDERAL RESPONSE 5 (Sept. 2011) [hereinafter PEER-TO-PEER VIOLENCE], http://www.usccr.gov/pubs/2011statutory.pdf.

rules. In the void that now exists, the U.S. Department of Education has provided some direction by way of "Dear Colleague Letters" and official guidance. This chapter will review those letters and the department's relevant guidance, as well as the bullying report of the U.S. Commission on Civil Rights.

A. Dear Colleague Letters

At the federal level, there are no statutes prohibiting bullying. However, the U.S. Department of Education has provided legal guidance to school districts about bullying using Dear Colleague Letters. The department has also issued Dear Colleague Letters with guidance concerning sexual and disability harassment. Although the Dear Colleague Letters are not formally adopted regulations, they represent the views of the department for purposes of enforcement of the laws within its jurisdiction.

1. Bullying Letters

On October 26, 2010, the Office for Civil Rights in the U.S. Department of Education issued a Dear Colleague Letter that was sent to all public school districts in the United States.[2] The purpose of this letter was to provide guidance

---

2. Office for Civil Rights, U.S. Dep't of Educ., Dear Colleague Letter (Oct. 26, 2010) (*re* harassment and bullying) [hereinafter Dear Colleague Letter: Harassment and Bullying], http://www2.ed.gov/about/offices/list/ocr/letters/colleague-201010.pdf. For the position of the National School Boards Association on this guidance, see Francisco M.

to school districts regarding what the Department of Education believes to be the obligation of the districts to address bullying as part of the districts' enforcement of existing federal laws and regulations. The letter began thus:

> In recent years, many state departments of education and local school districts have taken steps to reduce bullying in schools. The U.S. Department of Education (Department) fully supports these efforts. Bullying fosters a climate of fear and disrespect that can seriously impair the physical and psychological health of its victims and create conditions that negatively affect learning, thereby undermining the ability of students to achieve their full potential. The movement to adopt anti-bullying policies reflects schools' appreciation of their important responsibility to maintain a safe learning environment for all students. I am writing to remind you, however, that some student misconduct that falls under a school's anti-bullying policy also may trigger responsibilities under one or more of the federal antidiscrimination laws enforced by the Department's Office for Civil Rights (OCR). As discussed in more detail below, by limiting its response to a

Negrón Jr., Gen. Counsel, Nat'l Sch. Bds. Ass'n, Letter in Response to Dear Colleague Letter Issued October 26, 2010 (Dec. 7, 2010), http://www.nsba.org/SchoolLaw/Issues/Safety/NSBA-letter-to-Ed-12-07-10.pdf.

specific application of its anti-bullying disciplinary policy, a school may fail to properly consider
whether the student misconduct also results in
discriminatory harassment.[3]

The letter then provided guidance to school districts regarding the scope of harassment and how to address it:

Harassing conduct may take many forms, including verbal acts and name-calling; graphic and written statements, which may include use of cell
phones or the Internet; or other conduct that may
be physically threatening, harmful, or humiliating.
Harassment does not have to include intent to
harm, be directed at a specific target, or involve
repeated incidents. Harassment creates a hostile
environment when the conduct is sufficiently
severe, pervasive, or persistent so as to interfere
with or limit a student's ability to participate in or
benefit from the services, activities, or opportunities offered by a school. When such harassment is
based on race, color, national origin, sex, or disability, it violates the civil rights laws that OCR
enforces.

A school is responsible for addressing harassment incidents about which it knows or reasonably
should have known. In some situations, harass-

---

3. Dear Colleague Letter: Harassment and Bullying, *supra* note 2.

ment may be in plain sight, widespread, or well-known to students and staff, such as harassment occurring in hallways, during academic or physical education classes, during extracurricular activities, at recess, on a school bus, or through graffiti in public areas. In these cases, the obvious signs of the harassment are sufficient to put the school on notice. In other situations, the school may become aware of misconduct, triggering an investigation that could lead to the discovery of additional incidents that, taken together, may constitute a hostile environment. In all cases, schools should have well-publicized policies prohibiting harassment and procedures for reporting and resolving complaints that will alert the school to incidents of harassment.

When responding to harassment, a school must take immediate and appropriate action to investigate or otherwise determine what occurred. The specific steps in a school's investigation will vary depending upon the nature of the allegations, the source of the complaint, the age of the student or students involved, the size and administrative structure of the school, and other factors. In all cases, however, the inquiry should be prompt, thorough, and impartial.

If an investigation reveals that discriminatory harassment has occurred, a school must take prompt and effective steps reasonably calculated to end the harassment, eliminate any hostile environment and its effects, and prevent the harassment from recurring. These duties are a school's responsibility even if the misconduct also is covered by an anti-bullying policy, and regardless of whether a student has complained, asked the school to take action, or identified the harassment as a form of discrimination.

Appropriate steps to end harassment may include separating the accused harasser and the target, providing counseling for the target and/or harasser, or taking disciplinary action against the harasser. These steps should not penalize the student who was harassed. For example, any separation of the target from an alleged harasser should be designed to minimize the burden on the target's educational program (e.g., not requiring the target to change his or her class schedule).

In addition, depending on the extent of the harassment, the school may need to provide training or other interventions not only for the perpetrators, but also for the larger school community, to ensure that all students, their families, and school staff can recognize harassment if it recurs and know how to respond. A school also may be required to provide additional services to the student who was harassed in order to address the effects of the harassment, particularly if the school initially delays in responding or responds inappropriately or inadequately to information about harassment. An effective response also may need to include the issuance of new policies against harassment and new procedures by which students, parents, and employees may report allegations of harassment (or wide dissemination of existing policies and procedures), as well as wide distribution of the contact information for the district's Title IX and Section 504/Title II coordinators.

Finally, a school should take steps to stop further harassment and prevent any retaliation against the person who made the complaint (or was the subject of the harassment) or against those who provided information as witnesses. At a minimum, the school's responsibilities include making sure that the harassed students and their families know how to report any subsequent problems, conducting follow-up inquiries to see if there have been any new incidents or any instances of retaliation, and responding promptly and appropriately to address continuing or new problems.[4]

---

4. *Id.*

This Dear Colleague Letter sparked a lively debate within the education community. On behalf of the National School Boards Association (NSBA), Francisco Negrón, general counsel, wrote to Russlynn Ali, OCR's assistant secretary, and raised several concerns.[5] In his December 7, 2010, letter, Negrón identified several areas of disagreement with the content of the Dear Colleague Letter:

- Citing the U.S. Supreme Court decision in *Davis v. Monroe County Board of Education*,[6] Negrón noted that the Court imposed liability on school districts that "had actual knowledge" of harassment, but the Dear Colleague Letter stated that a school district was "responsible for addressing harassment incidents" not only "about which it knows" but also about which it "reasonably should have known."

- Negrón noted the difference between the conjunction used in the *Davis* requirement that harassment be "severe, pervasive, *and* objectively offensive" (emphasis supplied) and the disjunction used in the Dear Colleague Letter requirement that "[h]arassment creates a hostile environment when the conduct is sufficiently severe, pervasive, *or* persistent. . . ."

- Negrón viewed the Dear Colleague Letter as requiring school districts to "eliminate harassment and the hostile environment that it creates and to prevent it from occurring again" and contrasted that with the limited obligation of school districts under *Davis* to

---

5. Negrón, *supra* note 2.
6. 526 U.S. 629 (1999).

respond to harassment in a way that is not clearly unreasonable.[7]

NSBA also noted its concern that OCR's suggestions for remedial measures do not draw upon the education, experience, judgment, and personal knowledge of educators; that they may be impractical or impossible to implement; and that they may even violate the Family Educational Rights and Privacy Act.[8] Finally, Negrón pointed out to OCR that it gave very little consideration to the First Amendment issues that permeate the regulation of bullying, particularly when the bullying occurs off campus.[9]

Ali responded to NSBA in a letter dated March 25, 2011.[10] In her response, she stated that OCR disagreed with NSBA's contentions regarding the Dear Colleague Letter and said, in essence, that NSBA had misread the letter. According to Ali, the standards set forth in the Dear Colleague Letter are ones that OCR has used in previous guidance (such as the 2001 Sexual Harassment Guidance) and that reflect the enforcement position of OCR as opposed to OCR's statement of the law.

The debate regarding this Dear Colleague Letter has not been confined to NSBA and OCR. At the U.S. Commis-

---

7. Negrón, *supra* note 2, at 2–3.
8. *Id. at* 3–6.
9. *Id.* at 6–7.
10. Russlynn Ali, Assistant Sec'y for Civil Rights, U.S. Dept. of Education Office for Civil Rights, Letter in Response to Letter of Francisco M. Negrón Jr. Dated December 7, 2010 (Mar. 25, 2011), http://www.nsba .org/SchoolLaw/Issues/Equity/ED-Response-to-NSBA-GCs-Letter-to-ED- on-OCR-Bullying-Guidelines.pdf.

sion on Civil Rights Briefing on the Federal Response to
Peer-to-Peer Violence and Bullying[11] held on May 13, 2011,
and in various statements and comments via various other
venues, a number of speakers added their input, some challenging and some supporting the positions taken by OCR.

Some of the presenters who challenged OCR included
the following:

- Eugene Volokh, Professor, University of California,
  Los Angeles:

    I would caution against policies that are written
    using vague terms such as "bullying," "harass-
    ment," or "hostile educational environment,"
    especially when the policies cover speech that
    isn't targeted to a particular person, as well as
    speech that is said off-campus.[12]

- Kenneth L. Marcus, Executive Vice President and
  Director, Anti-Semitism Initiative, Institute for Jew-
  ish & Community Research:

    OCR's failure to recognize First Amendment lim-
    itations is particularly conspicuous in its new
    policy document, given the aggressive position
    that it is taking on the legal standards for estab-
    lishing harassment. To the extent that OCR will

---

11. *The Federal Response to Peer-to-Peer Violence and Bullying:
Briefing Before the U.S. Comm'n on Civil Rights* (May 13, 2011) [here-
inafter *Briefing*], http://www.eusccr.com/Peer-Bullying%20May%2013%
202011%20Transcript.pdf.

12. Peer-to-Peer Violence, *supra* note 1, at 76 n.371 (quoting
http://www.eusccr.com/27.%20Eugene%20Volokh,%20UCLA%20School%
20of%20Law.pdf).

find harassment in single-incident cases of offensive speech which are merely "severe, pervasive *or* persistent," First Amendment concerns will inevitably arise.[13]

- Neal McCluskey, Associate Director, Center for Educational Freedom, Cato Institute:

  While much that is called bullying and harassment is no doubt behavior intended to threaten or intimidate, identifying motive can be very difficult, and empowering government-employed educators to decide what behavior or speech is intended to harass or intimidate, rather than to express and [*sic*] an opinion, is dangerous.[14]

- Hiram S. Sasser III, Director of Litigation, Liberty Institute:

  It is tempting to engage in censorship of some students to benefit others, but the cause of freedom is never advanced by selective censorship of those messages with which the government disagrees.[15]

- National Coalition Against Censorship:

  By stretching the definition of harassment to encompass various kinds of interactions in schools

---

13. *Id.* (quoting http://www.eusccr.com/15.%20Kenneth%20L.%20 Marcus,%20Institute%20for%20Jewish%20&%20Community%20 Research.pdf (citation omitted) (emphasis in original)).

14. *Id.* (quoting http://www.eusccr.com/28.%20Neal%20McCluskey, %20Cato%20Institute.pdf).

15. *Id.* (quoting http://www.eusccr.com/11.%20Hiram%20S.%20 Sasser,%20III,%20Liberty%20Institute.pdf).

and colleges, the letter threatens the delicate balance the Supreme Court has struck between the right to equality at work and school and the right to free speech, an approach reflected in OCR pronouncements until recently.[16]

The following were among the number of speakers who supported OCR:

- Lambda Legal:

    [S]tudent speech has bounds, especially when it truly—not speculatively—disrupts a school's functioning or interferes with the rights of other students to secure the full range of educational advantages and benefits that are their due.[17]

- Eliza Byard, Executive Director, Gay Lesbian, and Straight Education Network:

    But let me be very clear: the words faggot and dyke are not part of any religious creed. And harassment and assault are crimes. . . . [The definition for bullying and harassment] includes the concept that the student has a reasonable fear of physical harm, as a result of what they are facing, and even a word as ugly as faggot or dyke . . . has to be used in a context where it produces that expectation in a

---

16. *Id.* at 77 n.371 (quoting http://www.scribd.com/doc/56492194/Comments-on-Federal-Anti-Bullying-Policy-on-Free-Expression).

17. *Id.* at 81 n.392 (quoting http://www.eusccr.com/Lambda%20Legal.pdf).

student in order to constitute bullying, or to constitute harassment.[18]

- Ilan Meyer, Professor, Columbia University:

  [N]othing in my testimony . . . is about speech at all. What I was talking about is about schools supporting affirmatively a gay student . . . against the types of evidence . . . about being injured, about physical assault, about rape, about being threatened, about having their property stolen, about being threatened with a knife or a weapon.[19]

- Erwin Chemerinsky, Dean, Irvine School of Law, University of California:

  Schools may prohibit all conduct, including speech, that constitutes harassment or threats on the basis of characteristics such as race, gender, religion and sexual orientation. The more speech is simply the expression of ideas, even offensive ideas, the greater the likelihood that it is protected by the First Amendment. However, courts recognize the need for schools to protect their students from harassment and courts are thus likely to be very deferential to school officials in deciding when speech is harassment or threats that can be prohibited and punished.[20]

---

18. *Briefing, supra* note 11, at 90, 135.

19. *Id.* at 125–26.

20. PEER-TO-PEER VIOLENCE, *supra* note 1, at 84 n.407 (quoting http://www.euscc.com/Chemerinsky%20-%20KTolhurst%20Ltr%20011-0523.pdf).

In light of the strong sentiments that were expressed before the commission, it is not likely that the debate concerning the October 26, 2010, Dear Colleague Letter will soon subside.

2. Peer Sexual Harassment and Sexual Violence Letters

On April 4, 2011, another Dear Colleague Letter was issued, this time focused on peer sexual harassment and sexual violence.[21] Although the letter dealt with issues that are perhaps more likely to occur at the postsecondary level, it was explicitly applicable to elementary and secondary schools in addition to colleges and universities.

The letter reviewed in detail the existing obligations of school districts under Title IX of the Education Amendments of 1972,[22] and it supplemented the previous guidance of the department concerning sexual harassment that was issued in 2001.[23]

OCR summarized the obligations of school districts under Title IX as follows:

---

21. Office for Civil Rights, U.S. Dep't of Educ., Dear Colleague Letter (Apr. 4, 2011) (*re* sexual violence) [hereinafter Dear Colleague Letter: Sexual Violence], http://www2.ed.gov/about/offices/list/ocr/letters/colleague-201104.pdf.

22. 20 U.S.C. §§ 1681 *et seq.*

23. OFFICE FOR CIVIL RIGHTS, U.S. DEP'T OF EDUC., REVISED SEXUAL HARASSMENT GUIDANCE: HARASSMENT OF STUDENTS BY SCHOOL EMPLOYEES, OTHER STUDENTS, OR THIRD PARTIES; TITLE IX (Jan. 2001) [hereinafter REVISED SEXUAL HARASSMENT GUIDANCE], http://www2.ed.gov/about/offices/list/ocr/docs/shguide.pdf.

If a school knows or reasonably should know about student-on-student harassment that creates a hostile environment, Title IX requires the school to take immediate action to eliminate the harassment, prevent its recurrence, and address its effects. Schools also are required to publish a notice of nondiscrimination and to adopt and publish grievance procedures. Because of these requirements, which are discussed in greater detail in the following section, schools need to ensure that their employees are trained so that they know to report harassment to appropriate school officials, and so that employees with the authority to address harassment know how to respond properly. Training for employees should include practical information about how to identify and report sexual harassment and violence. OCR recommends that this training be provided to any employees likely to witness or receive reports of sexual harassment and violence, including teachers, school law enforcement unit employees, school administrators, school counselors, general counsels, health personnel, and resident advisors.[24]

The obligations described in the Dear Colleague Letter are not limited to activities take place on campus. The let-

---

24. Dear Colleague Letter: Sexual Violence, *supra* note 21, at 4.

ter expanded the scope of its reach to include off-campus activity that has the effect of creating a hostile environment on campus:

> Schools may have an obligation to respond to student-on-student sexual harassment that initially occurred off school grounds, outside a school's education program or activity. If a student files a complaint with the school, regardless of where the conduct occurred, the school must process the complaint in accordance with its established procedures. Because students often experience the continuing effects of off-campus sexual harassment in the educational setting, schools should consider the effects of the off-campus conduct when evaluating whether there is a hostile environment on campus. For example, if a student alleges that he or she was sexually assaulted by another student off school grounds, and that upon returning to school he or she was taunted and harassed by other students who are the alleged perpetrator's friends, the school should take the earlier sexual assault into account in determining whether there is a sexually hostile environment. The school also should take steps to protect a student who was assaulted off campus from further sexual harassment or retaliation from the perpetrator and his or her associates.[25]

---

25. *Id.*

The Dear Colleague Letter did not draw a distinction between off-campus conduct and speech. Thus, a fair interpretation of its guidance is that school districts must respond to and act upon a complaint even if the complaint is limited to e-mails, text messages, Facebook posts, and Tweets, provided those communications constitute sexual harassment.

The Title IX grievance procedures are applicable to claims of bullying that fall within the scope of Title IX, and the Dear Colleague Letter discussed those procedures at length.[26] In addition to providing notice of the grievance procedures and providing an adequate, reliable, and impartial investigation, school districts are required to specify the time frame for all major steps of the grievance procedure. OCR noted that a typical investigation will take approximately sixty calendar days. The letter stated that the procedures must provide that notice of the outcome be given to both parties and that the parties be apprised of their right to appeal.

The Dear Colleague Letter included recommendations for steps to prevent harassment and violence, and it emphasized education and prevention. Among the educational recommendations were the following:

> Schools may want to include these education programs in their (1) orientation programs for new students, faculty, staff, and employees; (2) training for students who serve as advisors in residence

---

26. *Id.* at 8–14.

halls; (3) training for student athletes and coaches; and (4) school assemblies and "back to school nights." These programs should include a discussion of what constitutes sexual harassment and sexual violence, the school's policies and disciplinary procedures, and the consequences of violating these policies.[27]

In its lengthy discussion of remedies and enforcement, OCR identified remedies for both the specific students involved in a complaint proceeding as well as for the broader student body. The student-specific remedies cited by OCR were as follows:

- providing an escort to ensure that the complainant can move safely between classes and activities;
- ensuring that the complainant and alleged perpetrator do not attend the same classes;
- moving the complainant or alleged perpetrator to a different residence hall or, in the case of an elementary or secondary school student, to another school within the district;
- providing counseling services;
- providing medical services;
- providing academic support services, such as tutoring;

---

27. *Id.* at 14–15.

- arranging for the complainant to retake a course or withdraw from a class without penalty, ensuring that any changes do not adversely affect the complainant's academic record; and

- reviewing any disciplinary actions taken against the complainant to see if there is a causal connection between the harassment and the misconduct that may have resulted in the complainant being disciplined.[28]

3. Disability Harassment Letters

The Department of Education issued a Dear Colleague Letter concerning disability harassment in 2000.[29] This letter followed the principles set out in other department guidance concerning harassment in general, but it also provided examples of disability harassment that would be readily identified today as bullying:

> Disability harassment under Section 504 and Title II is intimidation or abusive behavior toward a student based on disability that creates a hostile environment by interfering with or denying a student's participation in or receipt of benefits, services, or opportunities in the institution's program. Harass-

---

28. *Id.* at 16–17.

29. Office for Civil Rights, U.S. Dep't of Education, Dear Colleague Letter (July 25, 2000) (*re* prohibited disability harassment), *available at* http://www2.ed.gov/about/offices/list/ocr/docs/disabharassltr.html.

ing conduct may take many forms, including verbal acts and name-calling, as well as nonverbal behavior, such as graphic and written statements, or conduct that is physically threatening, harmful, or humiliating.

When harassing conduct is sufficiently severe, persistent, or pervasive that it creates a hostile environment, it can violate a student's rights under the Section 504 and Title II regulations. A hostile environment may exist even if there are no tangible effects on the student where the harassment is serious enough to adversely affect the student's ability to participate in or benefit from the educational program. Examples of harassment that could create a hostile environment follow.

- Several students continually remark out loud to other students during class that a student with dyslexia is "retarded" or "deaf and dumb" and does not belong in the class; as a result, the harassed student has difficulty doing work in class and her grades decline.
- A student repeatedly places classroom furniture or other objects in the path of classmates who use wheelchairs, impeding the classmates' ability to enter the classroom.

- A teacher subjects a student to inappropriate physical restraint because of conduct related to his disability, with the result that the student tries to avoid school through increased absences.
- A school administrator repeatedly denies a student with a disability access to lunch, field trips, assemblies, and extracurricular activities as punishment for taking time off from school for required services related to the student's disability.
- A professor repeatedly belittles and criticizes a student with a disability for using accommodations in class, with the result that the student is so discouraged that she has great difficulty performing in class and learning.
- Students continually taunt or belittle a student with mental retardation by mocking and intimidating him so he does not participate in class.[30]

B. Guidance on Sexual Harassment

Under the authority granted to it by Title IX, the Department of Education issued sexual harassment guidance to

---

30. *Id.*

school districts in March of 1997.[31] Following the issuance of that guidance, the U.S. Supreme Court decided two Title IX cases involving the sexual harassment of students: *Gebser v. Lago Vista Independent School District*[32] and *Davis*, discussed earlier in this chapter. These cases prompted the department to issue new guidance in January of 2001—*Revised Sexual Harassment Guidance: Harassment of Students by School Employees, Other Students, or Third Parties; Title IX*—in which it summarized the rulings of these cases as follows:

> The Court held in *Gebser* that a school can be liable for monetary damages if a teacher sexually harasses a student, an official who has authority to address the harassment has actual knowledge of the harassment, and that official is deliberately indifferent in responding to the harassment. In *Davis*, the Court announced that a school also may be liable for monetary damages if one student sexually harasses another student in the school's program and the conditions of *Gebser* are met.[33]

In the context of bullying, the 2001 guidance is instructive with regard to the position of the department on cases of bullying that also fall under the category of sexual ha-

---

31. Sexual Harassment Guidance: Harassment of Students by School Employees, Other Students, or Third Parties, 62 Fed. Reg. 12,034 (Mar. 1997).

32. 524 U.S. 274 (1998).

33. REVISED SEXUAL HARASSMENT GUIDANCE, *supra* note 23, at ii.

rassment. As a general proposition, the department spoke specifically to student-on-student harassment and said thus:

> If a student sexually harasses another student and the harassing conduct is sufficiently serious to deny or limit the student's ability to participate in or benefit from the program, and if the school knows or reasonably should know about the harassment, the school is responsible for taking immediate effective action to eliminate the hostile environment and prevent its recurrence. As long as the school, upon notice of the harassment, responds by taking prompt and effective action to end the harassment and prevent its recurrence, the school has carried out its responsibility under the Title IX regulations. On the other hand, if, upon notice, the school fails to take prompt, effective action, the school's own inaction has permitted the student to be subjected to a hostile environment that denies or limits the student's ability to participate in or benefit from the school's program on the basis of sex. In this case, the school is responsible for taking effective corrective actions to stop the harassment, prevent its recurrence, and remedy the effects on the victim that could reasonably have been prevented had it responded promptly and effectively.[34]

---

34. *Id.* at 12 (citations omitted).

The actions that the department expects school districts to take in cases of sexual harassment closely mirror the actions required under bullying statutes and should serve as an added incentive for such action.

Since a number of bullying cases have involved students who have been victimized due to their sexual orientation, it is noteworthy that the department addressed this question as well:

> Although Title IX does not prohibit discrimination on the basis of sexual orientation, sexual harassment directed at gay or lesbian students that is sufficiently serious to limit or deny a student's ability to participate in or benefit from the school's program constitutes sexual harassment prohibited by Title IX under the circumstances described in this guidance. For example, if a male student or a group of male students target a gay student for physical sexual advances, serious enough to deny or limit the victim's ability to participate in or benefit from the school's program, the school would need to respond promptly and effectively, as described in this guidance, just as it would if the victim were heterosexual. On the other hand, if students heckle another student with comments based on the student's sexual orientation (e.g., "gay students are not welcome at this table in the cafeteria"), but

their actions do not involve conduct of a sexual nature, their actions would not be sexual harassment covered by Title IX.[35]

As previously noted, the 2001 guidance has been supplemented by the April 4, 2011, Dear Colleague Letter regarding peer sexual harassment and violence.[36] With the continuing press for more direction, it is likely that the department will issue additional guidance concerning this subject in the future.

C. U.S. Commission on Civil Rights Report on Bullying

On May 13, 2011, the U.S. Commission on Civil Rights held a briefing on student violence. The commission issued its report of these proceedings in September of 2011 in a document entitled *Peer-to-Peer Violence and Bullying: Examining the Federal Response.*[37] By way of introduction to the report, the commission observed that

[f]ederal civil rights laws—and the federal government's enforcement of those laws—are limited to heightened incidents of harassment that do not include typical schoolyard bullying unless that bul-

---

35. *Id.* at 3 (citations omitted).
36. Dear Colleague Letter: Sexual Violence, *supra* note 21.
37. PEER-TO-PEER VIOLENCE, *supra* note 1.

lying creates a hostile environment. As such, incidents of bullying reported in surveys and statistical
studies in this report do not necessarily meet the
threshold for federal jurisdiction.[38]

The report contained a comprehensive review of the information compiled by the commission at its briefing and
included the vote of the commission on August 21, 2011, to
support the following findings:

1. Bullying and harassment, including bullying and
   harassment based on sex, race, national origin,
   disability, sexual orientation, or religion, are
   harmful to American youth.
2. Current federal civil rights laws do not provide
   the U.S. Department of Education with jurisdiction to protect students from peer-to-peer
   harassment that is solely on the basis of religion.
3. The current federal civil rights laws do not protect students from peer-to-peer harassment that
   is solely on the basis of sexual orientation.[39]

The commission also voted in favor of six recommendations, including one (#5) specifically directed to OCR and
its October 26, 2010, Dear Colleague Letter:

---

38. *Id.* at 5.
39. *Id.* at 88.

1. The U.S. Departments of Education and Justice should track their complaints/inquiries regarding peer-to-peer harassment separately from complaints/inquiries regarding staff-to-student harassment.

2. The U.S. Departments of Education and Justice should track their complaints/inquiries regarding sexual harassment or gender-based harassment by creating a category that explicitly encompasses LGBT youth.

3. The U.S. Departments of Education and Justice should track complaints that they receive regarding harassment based solely on sexual orientation that are closed for lack of jurisdiction.

4. The U.S. Department of Education should track complaints that it receives regarding harassment based solely on religion that are closed for lack of jurisdiction.

5. The U.S. Department of Education should consider issuing a new Dear Colleague Letter regarding the First Amendment implications of anti-bullying policies. The new Letter should provide concrete examples to clarify the guidance that the Department of Education previously provided in its Dear Colleague Letter on the First Amendment dated July 28, 2003.

6. The U.S. Department of Education should strive to use consistent language when it articulates legal standards, such as its enforcement standards, in its Dear Colleague Letters and guidance documents. When the Department of Education uses different, even if consistent, terms in its Dear Colleague Letters and guidance documents, it should explain the reasoning behind its use of different wording.[40]

The brevity and limited nature of these findings and recommendations seem to be a reflection of the division within the commission. The commission's report was 217 pages long, but only 89 of those pages were devoted to the data and position statements presented to the commission at its briefing. The statements and rebuttals of the commissioners comprised the remaining 128 pages of the report. Commissioners Todd Gaziano and Peter Kirsanow submitted a 63-page dissent and rebuttal statement (with which Commissioner Gail Heriot concurred), and Heriot submitted a 32-page dissenting statement.

Gaziano and Kirsanow challenged the commission's assumption that bullying is a widespread problem and were critical of the lack of data and analysis in support of the commission's findings and recommendations. These commissioners cautioned against federal intervention without more of a factual and legal basis for that intervention:

---

40. *Id.* at 88–89.

Pursuant to the Commission's organic statute, the purpose of its annual enforcement report is to study and critique the effectiveness of federal agency efforts to enforce one or more of the existing civil rights laws, but no serious attempt was made to critique the effectiveness of ED's or DOJ's efforts in the Commission report. The apparent purpose of this report is to condemn social behavior that includes teasing, eye-rolling, and exclusion among K-12 students. Yet, even if the report was an attempt to describe the negative social behavior of 6-18 year-old students that it often misleadingly labels "bullying," its uncritical reliance on flawed surveys, advocacy group claims, and a mish-mash of contradictory statistics does more to mislead than cast light on the matter. Congress expects the Commission to exercise a higher level of professionalism in the social sciences. We regret that the Commission failed to live up to this expectation.

Since its creation, a central purpose of the Commission has been to "gather facts instead of charges" and "sift out the truth from the fancies" in the hopes of providing findings and recommendations "which will be of assistance to reasonable men." To do so requires the Commission to be a careful and neutral arbiter of the competing (and sometimes complex) facts, issues and policy considerations at work. It can only accomplish this goal by avoiding the hype that the broader topic of bullying evokes (even if the enforcement agencies have not been as careful). Responsible and critical analysis is necessary to avoid ill-conceived policy recommendations or enforcement actions that have negative, unintended consequences.

The general topic of student teasing, bullying, and social exclusion is not within this Commission's jurisdiction. Even so, the Commission's report provides no reliable indication of whether any such behavior is on the rise, has declined, or has stayed about the same over time. The advent of social technologies alone is not an indicator that bullying is on the rise. Even if it is, the only matter relevant to the Commission's study of federal civil rights laws is whether K-12 schools are responding as they should when they learn of severe and pervasive acts of bullying on the basis of protected classes that rises to the level of legally actionable harassment under the civil rights laws enforced by ED's Office for Civil Rights (OCR) and DOJ.

There also are significant statutory, First Amendment, and practical issues worthy of more careful and detailed discussion throughout the report rather than the cursory fashion in its last chapter. The issues involved in student-on-student harassment are not simple. Though it is emotionally appealing for some to join the chorus that a larger federal role would somehow bring the number of bullying incidents among 55 million K-12 students significantly down, the Commission must refrain from doing so absent more careful, detailed analysis.[41]

Gaziano and Kirsanow also contended that federal intervention in the regulation of bullying in school districts may be counterproductive and cited five reasons in support of their contention:

- First, increased federal pressure will inevitably increase the number of "zero tolerance" responses to alleged harassment with ridiculous results. . . .
- Second, expanded federal authority to investigate incidents of K-12 school bullying will divert federal attention from the rare but serious cases in which a particular school or school district really is indifferent to protected-class-based violence. . . .
- Third, greater federal regulatory involvement to prevent teasing and the like that doesn't rise to the level of what the Supreme Court defined as prohibited federal harassment will undercut the accountability local school officials and state legislators have to parents and students to prevent and address all types and degrees of bullying. . . .

41. *Id.* at 128–30.

- Fourth, as Commissioner Heriot demonstrated in her accompanying dissent and we explained during the Commission's May 13 briefing, 800-pound gorillas from Washington, DC tend to get their way, but their ways are not always best. One-size-fits-all rules and wrongheaded ideas from Washington may have various counterproductive effects. . . .

- Fifth, one of the zero tolerance responses worthy of special note is that the "antibullying" indoctrination called for by many of the activists may violate freedom of conscience and actually teach intolerance, instead of meaningful tolerance of differing opinions. . . .[42]

On the other side of the issue, Commissioner Roberta Achtenberg argued that the data provided to the commission supports twelve additional findings.[43] Achtenberg also made the following fourteen specific recommendations for action at the federal, state, and local levels:

Recommendation #1: Involved federal agencies, including the U.S. Department of Justice and the U.S. Department of Education, should provide funding for additional research into the seriousness, pervasiveness, and impact of peer-to-peer bullying, harassment, and violence, including

---

42. *Id.* at 164–67 (internal citations omitted).
43. *Id.* at 100–123.

cyberbullying, targeted toward students due to their race, national origin, sex, disability, religion, and/or sexual minority or gender non-conforming status in schools in the United States.

Recommendation #2: Additional scholarly research should examine with as much specificity as possible the issues of seriousness, pervasiveness, and impact of peer-to-peer bullying, harassment, and violence for students targeted due to their race, national origin, sex, disability, religion, and/or sexual minority or gender non-conforming status.

Recommendation #3: The U.S. Department of Education and other relevant agencies should assist school districts in providing information to students and their families about the modalities, including cyberbullying, through which students target each other for bullying, harassment, or violence due to race, national origin, sex, disability, religion, and/or sexual minority or gender non-conforming status.

Recommendation #4: As the Centers for Disease Control and Prevention of the U.S. Department of Health and Human Services recommend, "[e]ffective state and local public health and school health policies and practices should be developed to help reduce the prevalence of health-risk behaviors and improve health outcomes among sexual minority youths. In addition, more state and local surveys designed to monitor health-risk behaviors and selected health outcomes among population-based samples of students in grades 9-12 should include questions on sexual identity and sex of sexual contacts."

Recommendation #5: Federal law enforcement agencies should collaborate with state and local law enforcement to ensure that the protections afforded under the Matthew Shepard and James Byrd, Jr. Hate Crimes Prevention Act to victimized students are, in fact, utilized fully and appropriately (including the requirement for collection of data regarding hate crimes both perpetrated by and against juveniles).

Recommendation #6: State governments should consider, as appropriate, either enacting anti-bullying statutes of the type put forth in the Anti-Defamation League's Model Statute "Cyber-bullying Prevention Law" or amending their existing anti-bullying statutes to conform with the parameters of this Model Statute. Localities and school districts would be well-advised to contemplate the comprehensive facets of this Model Statute when considering their own laws, regulations, and policies.

Recommendation #7: School districts should ensure that they are in compliance with federal laws and U.S. Department of Education guidance documents regarding the protection of students targeted for discriminatory peer-to-peer violence.

Recommendation #8: School districts should ensure appropriate training to enable staff to recognize and act to minimize students' animus-based behaviors toward each other.

Recommendation #9: School districts should provide to student victims and their families information about how to report incidents of violence, harassment and bullying, and how to enforce their rights, in a manner which is not unduly complicated, and which is written at a level (and in a language) easily comprehensible to students and their families.

Recommendation #10: School districts should ensure that the families of students are informed, in a timely manner and one which is respectful of student safety, when their children are subject to violence, harassment and bullying at school. Such parental notice may be especially important with regard to disabled students who are victimized, as these students may be unable to report the abuse to their families if unaided by school officials. This notice should be in language and manner comprehensible to the family, especially in the case of Limited English Proficiency families.

Recommendation #11: School districts should rescind existing "neutrality policies," "sexual orientation curriculum policies," and any directives which preclude or chill staff from discussing issues regarding homosexuality with students and their families, thereby allowing peer-to-peer violence, bullying, and harassment against sexual minority and gender non-conforming youth to go unaddressed.

Recommendation #12: Congress should enact, and the President should sign into law, the Safe Schools Improvement Act for the benefit of students targeted for peer-to-peer bullying, harassment, and violence due to race, national origin, sex, disability, sexual orientation, gender identity, or religion.

Recommendation #13: Congress should enact, and the President should sign into law, the Student Non-Discrimination Act for the benefit of students targeted for peer-to-peer bullying, harassment, and violence due to their sexual minority or gender non-conforming status.

Recommendation #14: Congress should enact, and the President should sign into law, an amendment Title VI of the Civil Rights Act of 1964 to prohibit discrimination on the basis of religion.[44]

Readers should review the complete text of this report and pay particular attention to the reasoned debate contained in the thoughtful statements of the commissioners.

---

44. *Id.* at 123–26 (citations omitted).

Suggestions for Dealing with Bullying

The typical school year in most states is about thirty-six weeks long. Students are in school for approximately forty hours for each of those thirty-six weeks. That means that the majority of students have about 1,440 hours of contact with their school each year. Those 1,440 hours translate into a lot of hours in which bullying can—and does—take place.

The issue has become prominent in society as incidents of violence and suicide due to bullying have become more common. And as the problem has escalated, the governments and the courts have responded to the problem. However, the legislative and judicial response is varied in its intensity and reach.

In order to effectively combat bullying, the issue needs to be addressed at other levels. On the home front, parents need to be educated about the issue. And on the school front, schools need to actively take steps to create a safe environment for students, including instituting policies that include good communication tactics and attention to cyberbullying issues.

A. Home Front

Although students are in school about 1,440 hours each year, it is important to note that there are 8,760 hours in a year. So, who watches over the children for the 7,320 non-school hours of the year? The point is that the issue of bullying is bigger than the schools and that it will take more than just the efforts of schools to address the issue.

Since parents have the primary responsibility for their children, they should not be ignored in efforts to combat bullying. Parents need to be made aware of the signs that their child might be the victim of bullying or that their child might be a bully. Stopbullying.gov lists these signs, and schools should share them with parents at the beginning of each school year. Signs that a child might be a victim include the following:

- Unexplainable injuries
- Lost or destroyed clothing, books, electronics, or jewelry
- Frequent headaches or stomachaches, sickness, or pretend illness
- Changes in eating habits, like suddenly skipping meals or binge eating (kids may come home from school hungry because they did not eat lunch)

- Difficulty sleeping or frequent nightmares
- Declining grades, loss of interest in schoolwork, or not wanting to go to school
- Sudden loss of friends or avoidance of social situations
- Feelings of helplessness or decreased self-esteem
- Self-destructive behaviors such as running away from home, harming self, or talking about suicide

Signs that a child might be a bully include the following:

- Getting into physical or verbal fights
- Having friends who bully others
- Becoming increasingly aggressive
- Getting sent to the principal's office or to detention frequently
- Having unexplained extra money or new belongings
- Blaming others for problems
- Not accepting responsibility for actions
- Becoming competitive and worrying about reputation or popularity[1]

Unfortunately, the effects of bullying may be quite severe, and each year a number of victims of bullying are lost to suicide. Schools should give parents the information that they

---

1. U.S. Dep't of Health and Human Services, stopbullying.gov, Warning Signs, http://www.stopbullying.gov/at-risk/warning-signs/index .html#bullied.

need so that they will know the warning signs of suicide. The National Suicide Prevention Lifeline lists these warning signs and has a toll-free number (1-800-273-8255) for further help:

- Talking about wanting to die or to kill oneself.
- Looking for a way to kill oneself, such as searching online or buying a gun.
- Talking about feeling hopeless or having no reason to live.
- Talking about feeling trapped or in unbearable pain.
- Talking about being a burden to others.
- Increasing the use of alcohol or drugs.
- Acting anxious or agitated; behaving recklessly.
- Sleeping too little or too much.
- Withdrawing or feeling isolated.
- Showing rage or talking about seeking revenge.
- Displaying extreme mood swings.[2]

B. School Front

Of course, the problem stretches beyond the reach of parents, and the terrifying reality that students may not be safe in school—whether they are being bullied there or are in the presence of victims who are acting out in response—was made vividly clear in Columbine and in other tragic

---

2. National Suicide Prevention Lifeline, What Are the Warning Signs for Suicide?, http://www.suicidepreventionlifeline.org/GetHelp/SuicideWarningSigns.aspx (last visited June 18, 2012).

cases. Although no one has yet found the ultimate solution, there are many suggestions for schools in dealing with the problem of bullying.

1. Government Publication

In 1999, the U.S. Department of Education and the U.S. Secret Service began working cooperatively to deal with the issue of school shootings and the relationship of school climate to those shootings. The result was a jointly produced publication entitled *Threat Assessment in Schools: A Guide to Managing Threatening Situations and to Creating Safe School Climates.*[3]

A safe school climate in which bullying is not tolerated is the product of a great deal of effort. The guide suggests eleven steps that schools and communities can take to begin to create a safe climate:

> *1. Assess the school's emotional climate.* Although no one wants to believe that this country's educational institutions are anything other than safe and positive environments that support the learning experience, it is incumbent upon those in positions of responsibility to take a "step back" and gain perspective on the emotional climate of their schools. This perspective can be gained by systematically

---

3. U.S. SECRET SERV. & U.S. DEP'T OF EDUC., THREAT ASSESSMENT IN SCHOOLS: A GUIDE TO MANAGING THREATENING SITUATIONS AND TO CREATING SAFE SCHOOL CLIMATES (2004), http://www2.ed.gov/admins/lead/safety/threatassessmentguide.pdf.

surveying students, faculty, and other important "stakeholders," such as parents, administrators, school board members, and representatives of community groups who interact with the school about the emotional climate of schools. Anonymous surveys, face-to-face interviews, focus groups, and psychological measures integrated into a total assessment package all have been used to varying degrees to gather key "real time" data. It is essential that school administrators, parents, and community leaders not assume that they know school climates as do those individuals—especially students—who are most directly affected by the educational experience on a daily basis. Absent a thorough assessment of climate process, school officials and leaders may never have the opportunity to find out what they did not know.

The findings of climate surveys can inform efforts to plan ways to enhance safety and respect within the educational environment. It is important to give feedback about school climate data to all involved and affected parties. Sharing climate data establishes a foundation for building an integrated systems approach that will bring the central "players" to the table; empower students to make change; and connect the school to the community and parental support.

2. Emphasize the importance of listening in schools. Pupils must listen respectfully to adults and to their peers, and teachers, administrators, and other adults must listen respectfully to their students and to each other. Grownups often expect that students listen to adults in authority. However, all too frequently adults forget that respectful listening is a "two-way street." A school with a culture of "two-way listening" will encourage and empower students to have the courage to break the ingrained code of silence.

Listening also must be expanded beyond academic concerns. Communications between teachers and students also should include listening to feelings, especially those of hurt and pain. In addition, it is important to "listen" to behaviors. Many students, including some who consider violence an appropriate way to solve problems, have a difficult time finding the words to articulate the disenfranchisement, hurt, or fear that they may feel. Not knowing how to express their problems and feelings may prompt these students to take action. Adults who listen to behavior and assist students in learning how to articulate their feelings and experiences provide students with critical skills that can contribute to preventing and reducing violence.

3. Take a strong, but caring stance against the code of silence. Silence leaves hurt unexposed and unacknowledged. Silence may encourage a young person to move along a path to violence.

4. Work actively to change the perception that talking to an adult about a student contemplating violence is considered "snitching." A school climate in which students connect to each other and to adults is one that promotes a safe and secure educational environment. A student who finds the courage to tell a caring adult about a friend in pain may save a life.

5. Find ways to stop bullying. Bullying is a continuum of abuse, ranging from verbal taunts to physical threats to dangerous acts. Bullying is not playful behavior. In bullying, one student assumes power by word or deed over another in a mean-spirited and/or harmful manner. In a school with a culture of safety and connection, both the bully and the student who is the victim of the bullying are attended to in a respectful manner. Schools with climates of safety and respect are establishing foundations for pro-social behavior. These climates teach conflict resolution, peer mediation, active listening, and other non-violent ways to solve problems. In a safe school climate, adults do not bully students and do not bully each other, and they do not turn a blind eye to bullying behavior when they know that it is going on in the school.

6. Empower students by involving them in planning, creating, and sustaining a school culture of safety and respect. Creating a safe school climate is a process that should involve all members of the school community, including teachers, students, parents, counselors, administrators, health staff, security professionals, and support personnel. Climates of safety should be collaborative ones. Helping students to engage in positive, productive activities or work in their local community can diminish isolation and enhance connection and safety.

7. Ensure that every student feels that he or she has a trusting relationship with at least one adult at school. Trusting relationships between adults and students are the products of quality connection, interaction, and communications. These relationships evolve and do not develop simply because an adult, such as a homeroom teacher or a guidance counselor, and a student have been ordered or assigned to interact with one another. Schools with cultures and climates of safety monitor students on a regular basis. School administrators should take steps to ensure that at least one adult at school knows what is happening with each student.

8. Create mechanisms for developing and sustaining safe school climates. A mechanism for developing and sustaining safe school climates should serve as a vehicle for planning and monitoring the climate and culture of the school. This mechanism may involve administrators, teachers, counselors, students, school law enforcement and security staff, and other personnel. Questions to be considered in implementing this mechanism might include: What should be done to develop and support climates of safety? To what extent are teachers, administrators, and other school staff encouraged to focus on students' social/emotional learning needs? How close is the school to achieving the goal of ensuring that every student feels that there is an adult to whom he or she can turn for talk, support, and advice if things get tough?

9. Be aware of physical environments and their effects on creating comfort zones. Building structure, facility safety plans, lighting, space, and architecture, among other physical attributes of educational institutions, all can contribute to whether a school environment feels, or is in fact, safe or unsafe. In large schools, school administrators may wish to explore changes in the physical characteristics of the school that would permit the assignment of teachers and students to smaller, mutually intersecting and supportive groupings within the broader educational community.

10. Emphasize an integrated systems model. People support most what they believe they have had genuine input in creating. This requires the difficult but necessary task of bringing all of the stakeholders to the table. Stakeholders include: students, teachers, administrators, school board members, parents, law enforcement personnel, after-school and community-based groups, and others. Stakeholders must struggle with questions such as the definition of "fairness," "threat," "consequence," and "change" as these concepts fit into the unique context of each school, school system, and the surrounding community.

11. All climates of safety ultimately are "local." Many local factors contribute to the creation of a culture and climate of safety. These factors include: the leadership–"open door" role of the school principal; "empowered buy-in" of student groups; connections to the local community and its leaders; and the respectful integration into the safe school climates process of "safekeepers," such as parents and law enforcement personnel close to the school.

Schools that have succeeded in creating safe school climates have done so because of their recognition that such climates of safety actually "raise the bar" on sound educational expectations, which, in turn, keep students engaged and learning at high levels. Such schools achieve their aims by realizing that safe school climates are not created overnight. Implementation of the safe school climates process requires planning and dedicated work. Participants in this process need adequate feedback and evaluative processes to sustain and continually improve educational environments. To work effectively, safe school climates that create relationships of respect and connection between adults and students must be accepted as integral to the mission of threat assessment and management, and understood from "the top down" as integral to the success of the learning experience.[4]

2. Author Recommendations

My own recommendations for addressing the problem of bullying begin with a policy. It is critical that every school district adopt a carefully drafted antibullying policy and complaint procedure that includes cyberbullying and complies with the constitutional restrictions arising from the First, Fourth, and Fourteenth Amendments. A good policy is one that has been thoroughly vetted not only by administrators, the school board, and the school attorney but also

---

4. *Id.* at 69–72 (emphasis in original).

by students, parents, teachers, and the broader community. That broader community should include any groups that advocate for the rights of students, whether those groups are based on a protected classification or on the rights of students as citizens. The policy must include complaint and investigation procedures and should provide for data reporting on a regular basis.

a. Communication

To be truly effective, the antibullying policy should focus on communication with and between the parties. It is not enough to investigate and punish an act of bullying. If the sole consequence for bullying is a period of suspension from school, it is highly likely that the school and the students and the parents will revisit the issue. Students and parents need to talk about the conduct and the communication that caused the problem, and they need to do so in some structured way.

One example of structured communication that might be helpful is a school-based peer mediation program using the standards proposed by the Association for Conflict Resolution[5] or a similar program focused on student-based problem solving. The policy may incorporate mediation as a means of dispute resolution even if mediation is not a part of the school's overall approach to bullying. Most victims just want the bullying to stop and want to be able to go to school in a safe environment. If requested by the victim, me-

---

5. *See* Ass'n for Conflict Resolution, Recommended Standards for School-Based Peer Mediation Programs 2007 (2007).

diation may be the best means of accomplishing those twin goals of the victim. The challenge with this approach is that it will require more resources and take more time, and it will only really work if the parties to the process are committed to making it work.

Although it is, of course, appropriate to focus most of the attention on the victim, it is also important to try to understand what motivated the bully and address the personal problems of the bully. Some bullies are themselves victims of bullying or victims of abuse. Punishment alone for bullies who have been bullied themselves and have learned this behavior from their own victimization is unproductive. School counselors or other behavior professionals should be involved in the problem-solving process.

b. Cyberbullying

Since a great deal of the bullying which occurs today is based on some form of electronic communication, schools should adopt a comprehensive policy regarding the use of electronic communication devices. This policy is separate from the anti-bullying policy but also serves to reinforce the goals of that policy. Students should be specifically advised in the policy that the possession and use of electronic communication devices in school is a privilege, not a right, and is subject to regulation by the school district. (In my review of the case law, I did not discover any appellate-level decision in any jurisdiction holding that students had a statutory or constitutional right to possess a cell phone or other electronic device in school.)

The policy regarding the possession and use of electronic communication devices should explicitly state that the student consents to the examination of the contents of the device by school officials as part of any investigation into allegations of misconduct. Compulsory production of security information has been the subject of a spate of recent legislation, mostly directed at employers. So, to the extent that some uses of electronic communication devices might be password-protected, the school district should consult with legal counsel to determine whether students can be compelled to reveal their passwords as part of an investigation.

The electronic communication device policy should specifically define the conduct that is unacceptable and identify the consequence for a violation. Schools should consider reducing or eliminating the penalty if the students participate in mediation and the mediation is successful from the point of view of the victim.

The policy should address the use of electronic communication devices outside of school where that use is directed toward or affects a student or staff member. If a student's off-campus use of an electronic communication device can be shown to have an on-campus effect that meets any one of the three standards of *Tinker* (material disruption of classwork or substantial disorder or interference with the rights of others), then the school should consider the full range of disciplinary options available to it. However, if the school cannot comfortably conclude that one of the three *Tinker* standards has been met, the penalty for off-campus violations should be limited to a limitation on the student's right to possess or use electronic communication devices at school.

Schools should develop and provide training to students regarding social and electronic communication etiquette, legal standards (e.g., sexting laws), and defensive tactics. Students today get their first phone long before they get their first car. Society demands that students be trained and licensed before they drive a vehicle, but it does not have similar expectations for the use of electronic communication devices. To be truly effective, schools should create a curriculum for the use of electronic communication devices and require completion of that curriculum before students can use the devices on campus. For decades, Drivers Ed has been an integral part of the educational system. There is no compelling reason why Talkers Ed, Texters Ed, Tweeters Ed, and Posters Ed should not likewise be a part of every student's education.

C. Final Words

The greatest danger in attacking the problem of bullying lies in the belief that words alone will make the problem go away. State legislatures have recognized the problem of bullying and have passed laws. School boards have recognized the problem of bullying and have adopted policies. Those words—the statutes and the policies—are important. But without more resources, all of those laws and policies are just that—words.

Index